Keep in touch!

Collins literacy email alerts keep you up to date with new primary literacy resources, downloads and competitions.

Make sure you don't miss out – sign up at:

www.collinseducation.com/emailalerts

Or tick the box below and send this form to our freepost address:

☐ I would like to sign up for Collins literacy email alerts

My email address is:

Name:

Address

Position

School

Postcode

Return to:

Annette Matthew, Collins Education, FREEPOST PAM6429, 77–85 Fulham Palace Road, London W6 8BR

Collins Big Cat.
Love Reading.

Collins Big Cat, the award-winning reading series for children aged 4+, provides exciting fiction and non-fiction books from top authors that children love. Evaluate Collins Big Cat for 30 days – simply tick the box below and return this form to our freepost address.

☐ Collins Big Cat Guided Reading evaluation pack   ISBN 0-00-776883-4 £90.00

☐ Collins Big Cat Phonics decodable readers evaluation pack   ISBN 0-00-777033-2 £20.00

Name:

Address

Position

School

Postcode

Return to:

Annette Matthew, Collins Education, FREEPOST PAM6429, 77–85 Fulham Palace Road, London W6 8BR

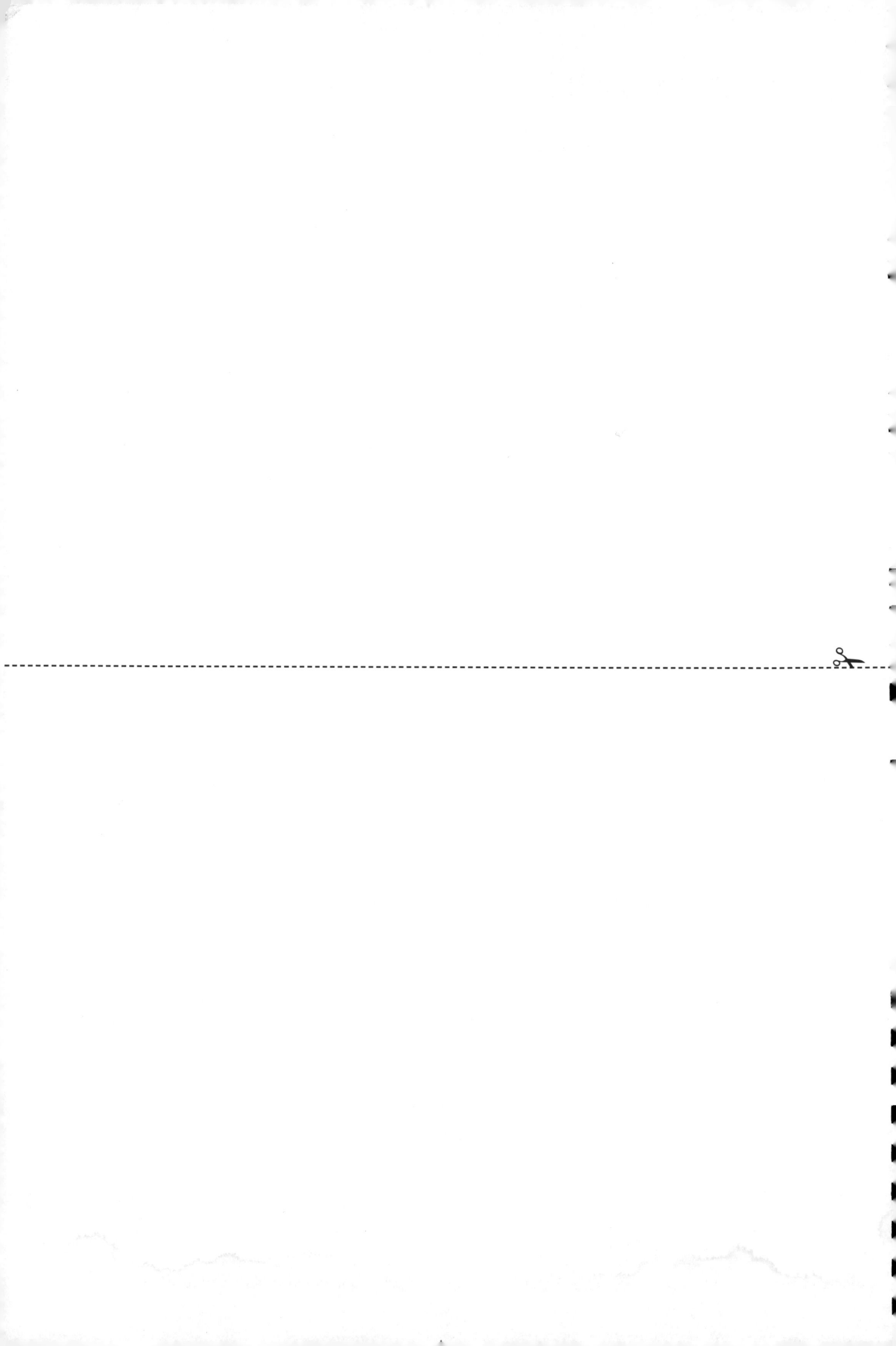

Collins Big Cat Phonics
Handbook

> It's so easy to use. It's foolproof. You can start the program on the whiteboard and just observe the class.
>
> **Earlswood Infant School**

> The consistent approach across year groups is vital for progression. Our standards in both reading and writing have risen as a consequence of the systematic approach.
>
> **Merland Rise Community Primary School**

Kay Hiatt

Collins

Collins Big Cat Phonics

William Collins' dream of knowledge for all began with the publication of his first book in 1819. A self-educated mill worker, he not only enriched millions of lives, but also founded a flourishing publishing house. Today, staying true to this spirit, Collins books are packed with inspiration, innovation and practical expertise. They place you at the centre of a world of possibility and give you exactly what you need to explore it.

Published by Collins
An imprint of HarperCollins*Publishers*
77–85 Fulham Palace Road
Hammersmith
London
W6 8JB

Browse the complete Collins catalogue at
www.collinseducation.com

© HarperCollins*Publishers* Limited 2006

Scottish advisor: Eleanor MacMillan

Author: Kay Hiatt

10 9 8 7 6 5 4 3 2

ISBN-13 978-0-00-723300-7
ISBN-10 0-00-723300-0

The author asserts her moral right to be identified as the author of this work

Any educational institution that has purchased one copy of this publication may make duplicate copies of pages 63–67 and 69–76, for use exclusively with that institution. Permission does not extend to reproduction, storage in a retrieval system, or transmission in any form or by any means – electronic, mechanical, photocopying, recording or otherwise – of duplicate copies for lending, renting or selling to any other institution without the prior consent, in writing, of the Publisher.

British Library Cataloguing in Publication Data
A catalogue record for this publication is available from the British Library

Acknowledgements
Collins would like to thank the teachers and children at the following schools who took part in the development of *Collins Big Cat Phonics*:
Anthony Bek Primary School
Earlswood Infant School
Englefield Green Infant School
Melcombe Primary School
Merton Abbey Primary School
Riverview Primary School

Designer: Neil Adams

Printed and bound by Martins the Printers, Berwick upon Tweed

Get the latest Collins Big Cat news at
www.collinsbigcat.com

Contents

A letter from Kay Hiatt   4

How to use this handbook   10

Collins Big Cat Phonics and the daily session   12

Collins Big Cat Phonics Readers   20

Collins Big Cat Phonics and learning objectives   30

Detailed programme outline   34

Collins Big Cat and synthetic phonics   55

Collins Big Cat Phonics and assessment   57

Activities   77

A Letter from Kay Hiatt

Author, *Collins Big Cat Phonics*

Dear Colleague,

As you know, the ability to read is fundamental to a child's success in school and later life. Any child in your class, whatever their background and experience, will be faced with the need to decode words in order to find meaning on the page, on screen, on signs or labels. Reading comprehension can't happen if a child can't decode. Fast, automatic decoding is the foundation for all reading – and supports success in writing too.

English is harder to read and spell than many other languages. Look at the long 'a' sounds and the 'er' sounds in these words:

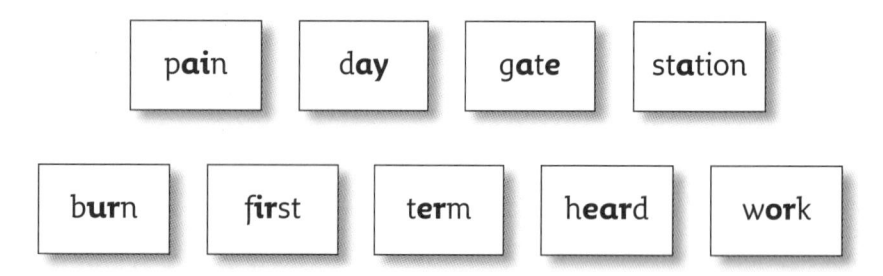

| pain | day | gate | station |

| burn | first | term | heard | work |

Children need to learn the relationship between sounds and letters in English because it is more complex than many other languages. They must be taught this relationship explicitly – it can't be left to chance. It needs to be taught as the main approach to reading – early, fast and systematically.

This systematic approach to matching sounds and letters really does work for young readers and writers. Set this approach into a language-rich, imaginative curriculum, and you offer every child the best chance of becoming a literate, confident adult, able to compete in society.

Systematic phonics

I'd like to share with you my experiences in teaching young children to read over several decades. I was lucky to have been taught how to teach reading and spelling effectively by an experienced infants' teacher in my first teaching post, in an inner city 'deprived' area. By the time the children had moved into my class, they were able to read simple books and attempt new words with confidence. Their previous teacher had taught them how to recognise and say many sounds, and how to use this knowledge to begin to blend along cvc words. She was using a system that is now described as synthetic phonics.

When the children were reading and met unknown words, I could hear and see them decoding and blending along words to read them. They drew upon these reading strategies rather than guessing words from the pictures.

My job as their teacher was to build upon and extend their phonic knowledge. A wider range of sounds were learned for blending along new words in their reading books. We also frequently 'read around the room', where they could read captions I had written (and changed regularly), and phonic charts.

This reading practice gave them the confidence and experience of reading fluently and accurately early on.

From speaking and listening to writing

To enrich the children's spoken language, I read books aloud to them, made up stories, told and retold fairy tales, acted out tales with them, and taught them rhymes and poems to recite together. This helped them to develop a more extensive vocabulary than most had started school with.

I started to ask more of the children in their writing. I asked them to have a go at writing anything from stories, to simple poems, to what they liked about school, encouraging them to sound out and segment any words they didn't know how to write. It took some time but, with lots of praise for having a go, it began to pay off.

Some years later I was involved in a project that looked closely at early writing development across a wide range of schools and settings. What surprised me was that large numbers of young children were not confident at moving on from 'play writing' into trying to represent words by initial letter sounds.

A good foundation of phonic knowledge gets results.

Closer analysis of the way these children were being taught revealed a very slow programme of teaching initial letter sounds, often taking a whole year to finish the alphabet. There was no continuing focus on the teaching and learning of sounds, taught alongside how to blend and segment words for spelling.

When you encourage children to attempt writing independently, right from their earliest 'mark-making' stage, you get a clear picture of what they know about writing. You can see at first hand the impact of phonics teaching as children begin to use the first sounds in words to represent the whole word. When a child has a good foundation of phonic knowledge and purposeful writing tasks that engage the child, good results are achieved. The examples on the following page show this.

Having enjoyed The Very Hungry Caterpillar *by Eric Carle, this five-year-old girl, who had been taught phonics in a systematic way, used her phonic knowledge to have a go at writing a shopping list for the caterpillar. She wrote this in the summer term, loved writing and went on to blossom in the next class.*

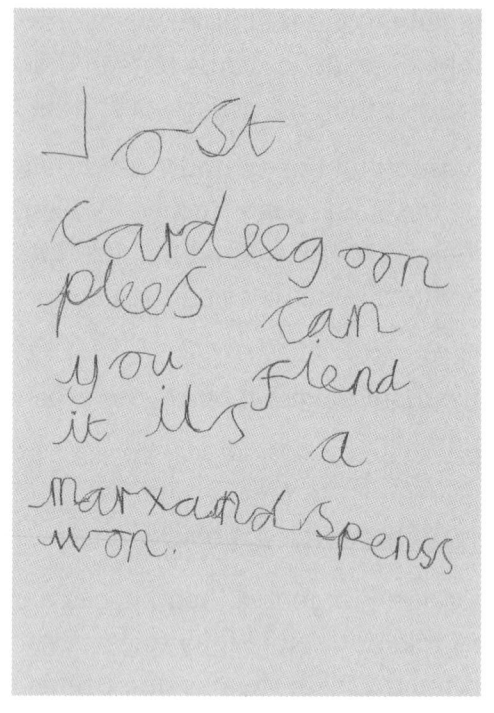

This was written by a five-year-old who had lost her cardigan and made this notice for the classroom door. It's a great example of a child writing for a real purpose!

Teaching children English as another language

I have often taught children who speak little or no English and have only just arrived in the UK. They learnt spoken English through active and interactive approaches: action rhymes, poems, picture stories, 'hands-on' science, maths, problem-solving approaches and small group work with English-speaking children.

From the beginning I taught them the English alphabet – letter names and sounds – and gave them plenty of blending and segmenting practice. They also learned a small bank of high-frequency words. Whatever they wrote, they read back to me, so that they quickly became used to the nature of phonics – what you segment, you need to then blend as you read. I noted that the experience of 'sounding out' words consolidated their reading skills. Their ability to decode allowed them to go on to consolidate their comprehension skills, through visual clues and discussion about the meaning of words across the curriculum, not just in literacy. This proved to me, yet again, the importance of having a rigorous approach to teaching reading and spelling.

Reading and enjoyment

Jim Rose's 2006 government review of early reading stresses, over and over, the importance of ensuring that the teaching of synthetic phonics sits comfortably *'within a broad and rich language curriculum: that is to say, a curriculum that generates purposeful discussion, interest, application, enjoyment and high achievement across all the areas of learning and experience in the early years and progressively throughout the key stages which follow.'*

Independent Review of the Teaching of Early Reading by Jim Rose CBE, March 2006

Reading and discussing books together will be a key experience for you and the children in your class, whether in shared, guided or paired reading. Discussion opens up the meaning of books for children and allows you to judge their understanding. It allows them to learn from other children's views and experiences.

Synthetic phonics fast and first

In my experience, those children who fail to thrive as readers and writers by the age of six are mainly those who have not yet secured a firm foundation of phonic knowledge. This results in low self-esteem, as increasingly wider gaps for attainment in reading and spelling become more and more obvious. Their ability to blend along words is poor; they often 'over-use' phonic strategies when attempting to read tricky words and tend to write very little. How children are taught to read in their first months at school can make all the difference to their later success.

Enjoying reading is a key experience for children.

A few years ago I decided to return to this crucial early stage of a child's school life and see what was happening in the classroom. Phonics was certainly back on the agenda, but although children were taught letter sounds in an active and interesting way, it took a long time, and often children were not getting daily practice of using this knowledge to blend along words. In addition, some low teacher expectation frequently led to the vowel digraphs (e.g. *ai*) included in popular schemes being left out until the following year 'when the children were ready'. Alarmingly, children were becoming increasingly dependent on using pictures alone as their main strategy for reading, rather than phonic-based decoding skills.

I became so concerned by what I saw that I developed a systematic, synthetic phonics programme which delivered a daily 10-minute session, and took this into many classrooms to train and work with teachers, with great success.

'The consistent approach across year groups, building on the skills which children have already developed, are vital for progression. Our standards in both reading and writing have risen as a consequence of the systematic approach to teaching phonics.'

Mrs Sally Leach, Headteacher, Merland Rise Community Primary School, Surrey.

Collins Big Cat Phonics

Collins Big Cat Phonics builds on and develops those successful strategies I used in schools, both in my own teaching and in training others.

It provides you with a carefully planned systematic way of teaching reading *and* writing through a daily 10-minute synthetic phonics session, using an electronic whiteboard or PC. Children quickly learn the main 42 sounds and how to blend and segment, with plenty of fast, fun daily practice so that the skills become automatic and are secured for life.

Big Cat and Snappy

A LETTER FROM KAY HIATT

A Collins Big Cat Phonics session in progress

Using *Collins Big Cat Phonics*, children learn how to pronounce each sound, how to blend and segment, and how to apply their knowledge to reading and writing. Children also learn a bank of irregular words which are hard to decode early on, e.g. *the*, *he* and *she*.

While the children learn with Big Cat and Snappy, you're able to observe individuals and assess how they're doing. Supportive assessment sheets and practical guidance on assessment are provided in this handbook.

The programme also includes a reading and writing section, which is great fun for the children, and which makes explicit the vital link between phonics, reading and writing. Nothing has been left to chance – everything you need to deliver has been planned, ready for you to use.

The daily *Collins Big Cat Phonics* session is delivered at a brisk pace with small learning steps, plenty of practice, and lots of success!

Kay Hiatt

How to use this handbook

Collins Big Cat Phonics Handbook provides teachers with practical teaching and assessment support, helping them to deliver a fast, systematic synthetic phonics programme that will give children the solid foundations they need to become successful readers and writers.

This handbook has five main sections:

A letter from Kay Hiatt – pages 4 to 9

Collins Big Cat Phonics author Kay Hiatt introduces *Collins Big Cat Phonics* and explains how it benefits the teaching of early reading and writing.

Structure and features – pages 12 to 19

This section outlines the content and structure of *Collins Big Cat Phonics*, including an overview of the five sections of the *Collins Big Cat Phonics* daily session – phoneme acquisition (Say), blending (Blend), segmenting (Chop), irregular words (Fast words) and reading and writing sentences (Read/Write).

Collins Big Cat Phonics and reading – pages 20 to 29

This section is a book-by-book guide, including planning notes, for the range of *Collins Big Cat Phonics Readers*, showing how they support *Collins Big Cat Phonics*.

Planning and teaching – pages 34 to 54

These pages are a practical planning tool, designed to help you quickly identify the right session for your class, group or child. They provide an at-a-glance outline of session content – with helpful tips and curriculum links.

Activities for further practice – pages 77 to 78

Here you can find out more about interactive activities that provide motivating practice for children's phonic skills.

HOW TO USE THIS HANDBOOK

If you feel confident about using synthetic phonics with your children, you could go straight to the session summaries on page 34.

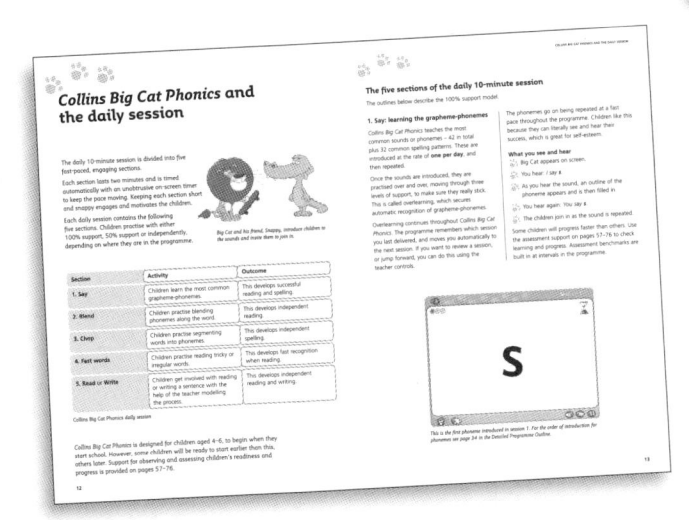

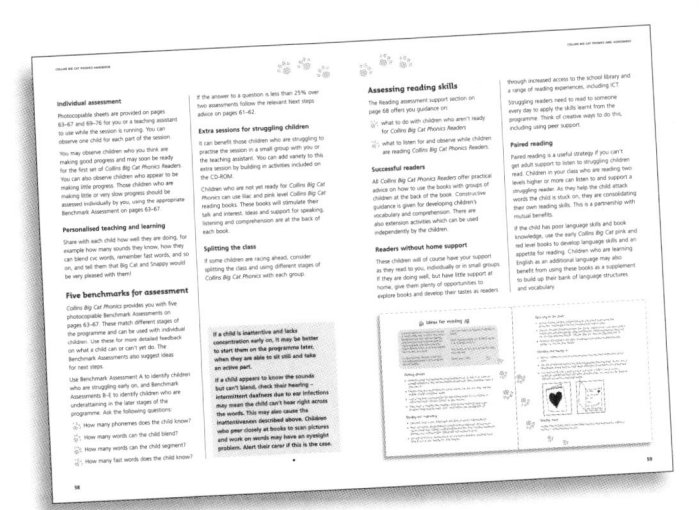

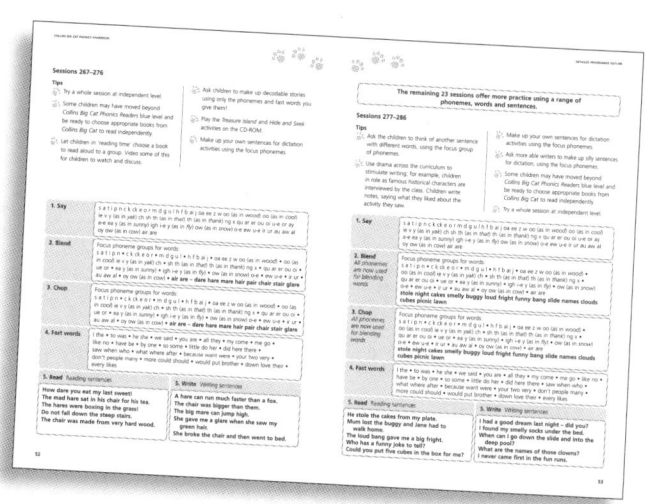

To learn more about *Collins Big Cat Phonics* and how it encourages the development of successful readers and writers, go to page 12.

For an overview of *Collins Big Cat Phonics Readers*, turn to page 20.

To look at a range of assessment techniques to help you identify the needs of individuals or groups, turn to page 57.

11

Collins Big Cat Phonics and the daily session

The daily 10-minute session is divided into five fast-paced, engaging sections.

Each section lasts two minutes and is timed automatically with an unobtrusive on-screen timer to keep the pace moving. Keeping each section short and snappy engages and motivates the children.

Each daily session contains the following five sections. Children practise with either 100% support, 50% support or independently, depending on where they are in the programme.

Big Cat and his friend, Snappy, introduce children to the sounds and invite them to join in.

Section	Activity	Outcome
1. Say	Children learn the most common grapheme-phonemes.	This develops successful reading and spelling.
2. Blend	Children practise blending phonemes along the word.	This develops independent reading.
3. Chop	Children practise segmenting words into phonemes.	This develops independent spelling.
4. Fast words	Children practise reading tricky or irregular words.	This develops fast recognition when reading.
5. Read or Write	Children get involved with reading or writing a sentence with the help of the teacher modelling the process.	This develops independent reading and writing.

Collins Big Cat Phonics *daily session*

Collins Big Cat Phonics is designed for children aged 4–6, to begin when they start school. However, some children will be ready to start earlier than this, others later. Support for observing and assessing children's readiness and progress is provided on pages 57–76.

The five sections of the daily 10-minute session

The outlines below describe the 100% support model.

1. Say: learning the grapheme-phonemes

Collins Big Cat Phonics teaches the most common sounds or phonemes – 42 in total plus 32 common spelling patterns. These are introduced at the rate of **one per day**, and then repeated.

Once the sounds are introduced, they are practised over and over, moving through three levels of support, to make sure they really stick. This is called overlearning, which secures automatic recognition of grapheme-phonemes.

Overlearning continues throughout *Collins Big Cat Phonics*. The programme remembers which session you last delivered, and moves you automatically to the next session. If you want to review a session, or jump forward, you can do this using the teacher controls.

The phonemes go on being repeated at a fast pace throughout the programme. Children like this because they can literally see and hear their success, which is great for self-esteem.

What you see and hear

- Big Cat appears on screen.
- You hear: *I say* **s**.
- As you hear the sound, an outline of the phoneme appears and is then filled in.
- You hear again: *You say* **s**.
- The children join in as the sound is repeated.

Some children will progress faster than others. Use the assessment support on pages 57–76 to check learning and progress. Assessment benchmarks are built in at intervals in the programme.

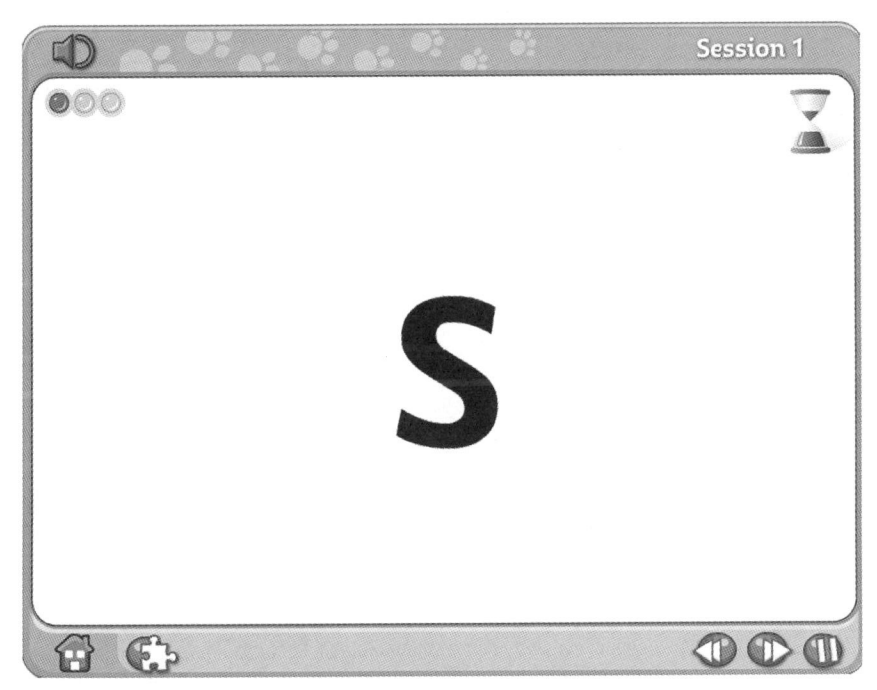

This is the first phoneme introduced in session 1. For the order of introduction for phonemes see page 34 in the Detailed Programme Outline.

2. Blend: blending phonemes along the word

What you see and hear

- Snappy appears on screen.
- You hear: *I say* **s-a-t – sat**.
- As you hear the word, an outline of the word appears and is then filled in.
- Sound buttons appear below each phoneme and blend into a line as the word is spoken.
- You hear again: *You say* **s-a-t – sat**.
- The children join in as the blending of the word is repeated.
- Many words are accompanied by an illustration which appears after the word has been blended/chopped by the children.

When the children join in, demonstrate how to use finger pointing. Finger pointing is when the child points at each sound button in turn, along the word. They then move their finger back to the beginning of the word, run their finger under the whole word and say it at the same time.

I tell children that blending sounds is like putting slices of peach, banana and strawberry into a blender and blending them together to make a smoothie. The fruits are blended together, in the same way that the sounds are blended to form words.

Blending for reading is further supported by *Collins Big Cat Phonics Readers*. These practise the phonemes introduced in the session. Turn to page 20 to see which books support each of the four stages.

Some children will progress faster than others. Use the assessment support on pages 57–76 to check learning and progress. Assessment benchmarks are built in at intervals in the programme.

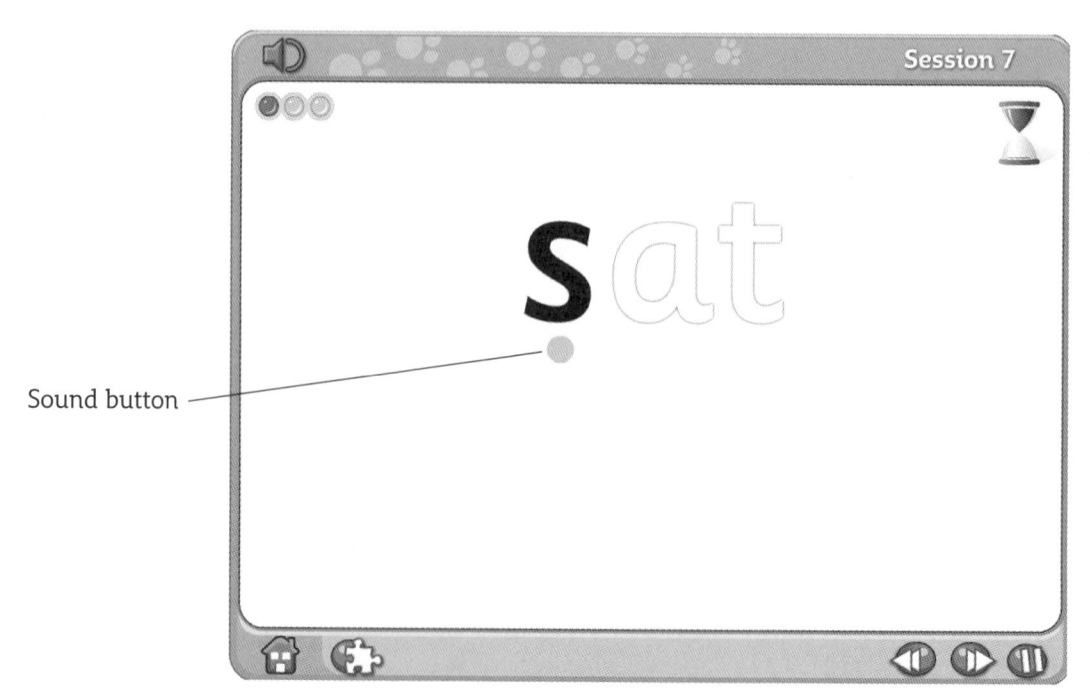

The word appears one phoneme at a time and is blended once all the phonemes are revealed.

3. Chop: segmenting words into phonemes

What you see and hear

- Big Cat appears on screen.
- You hear: *I say **snap** – **s-n-a-p**.*
- The word appears, one phoneme at a time, with sound buttons under each phoneme.
- You hear again: *You say **snap** – **s-n-a-p**.*
- There is a longer pause here while children chop the word up.
- This encourages visual and sound memory which is vital for spelling.
- Many words are accompanied by an illustration which appears after the word has been blended/chopped by the children.

Model finger counting and encourage the children to finger count with you every time. This is when they signal each phoneme by raising a finger, starting with their thumb. As they move along the word, they say the phonemes in the right order.

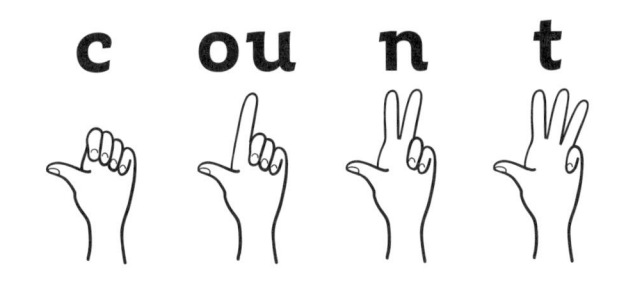

Finger counting

I tell children that good spellers can break a whole word into pieces, then write it correctly by putting the phonemes back together in the right order – just like breaking an orange into segments, then putting it back together again!

Some children will progress faster than others. Use the assessment support on pages 57–76 to check learning and progress. Assessment benchmarks are built in at intervals in the programme.

After hearing the word, the segmented word appears on the screen.

4. Fast words: reading irregular words

Some everyday words are irregular or hard to decode, for example 'the' and 'to'. These irregular words can't easily be sounded out. Teaching children a small number of irregular words as sight words helps them to become active readers quickly.

Collins Big Cat Phonics helps children learn a bank of irregular words at speed by teaching them to scan across the whole word. The 'picture' of the whole word is fixed into the visual memory and then recalled at speed. Children learn to recognise and say these words without any hesitation when they are reading. This technique is only used for a small number of irregular words. Regular, decodable high frequency words like 'dog' and 'get' are not included.

What you see and hear

- Snappy appears on screen.
- You hear: *I say* **the**.
- An outline of the word appears on screen and fills in as the word is spoken.
- You hear again: *You say* **the**.
- The children join in as the word is repeated.
- No sound buttons appear because the children should not attempt to blend or segment an irregular word.

An outline of the word appears on screen and fills in as the word is spoken.

5. Read *or* Write: reading or writing a sentence

Children practise reading and writing sentences on alternate days. This part of the session can be used with or without sound depending on your preference.

Modelling the reading process

- Each word in the sentence is covered up apart from the first word. It will either be decodable or a fast word the children have already learned.

- Say the whole word if it is not decodable, for example *the*. Tell the children that it is a fast word.

- If the first word is decodable, ask the children to blend along the word.

- Clicking on the blocks will reveal the words – phoneme by phoneme, for decodable words, and as a whole word for fast words. Encourage the class to blend along the word and then to say the whole word, e.g. *The (c-a-t) cat (s-a-t) sat (o-n) on the (the) (b-o-x) box.*

- Encourage the children to use other strategies, too, as you move along the sentence:

  – Can they predict which word might occur next, from the meaning of the sentence so far? (This supports their comprehension.)

  – Can they predict which word might occur next, from the order of words so far? (They use their early understanding of grammar to support them.)

- An illustration of the sentence appears when you select the green tick.

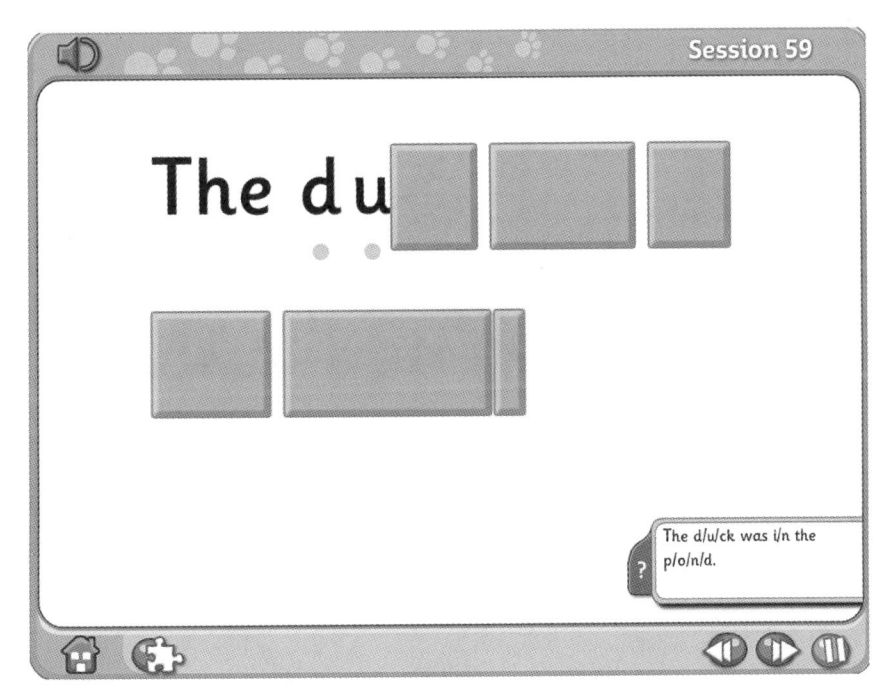

Reading sentences are revealed, as they are read.

Modelling the writing process

These two minutes are very important because the children see how to write, then read what has been written.

- The first screen is modelled automatically so children can see the forming of the letters and words.

- The next screen is blank other than a line to write on. Write the sentence, describing to the children what you are doing as follows.

- The segmented sentence can be found using the '?' tab at the right-hand side of the screen, if you need assistance.

- Ask the children to repeat the sentence with you.

- Ask them to count the words in the sentence using their fingers. Emphasise the terms *word* and *sentence* because some children may be confused about the difference between them.

- Say the first word of the sentence and ask the children to join in with you as you segment it into its phonemes. Model this by finger counting each phoneme as you say it, (holding up a finger for each phoneme starting with the thumb). Ask the children to use their fingers to count the sounds in the correct sequence along the word.

- If the first word is an irregular word, tell them it is a fast word and spell it out using **letter names**, not sounds.

- Write the word on the line in front of the children, making sure they can see how you are forming the letters.

- Continue in this way for the rest of the sentence.

- At regular intervals ask the children to re-read the words that you have written. The children are now blending instead of segmenting, practising both these crucial skills.

- Briefly talk about and show the correct punctuation for the sentence. Avoid asking the children what is correct, or asking them to come up to the whiteboard and punctuate. This will lengthen the session and some children will lose concentration. Remember – keep it snappy!

- An illustration of the sentence appears when you select the green tick.

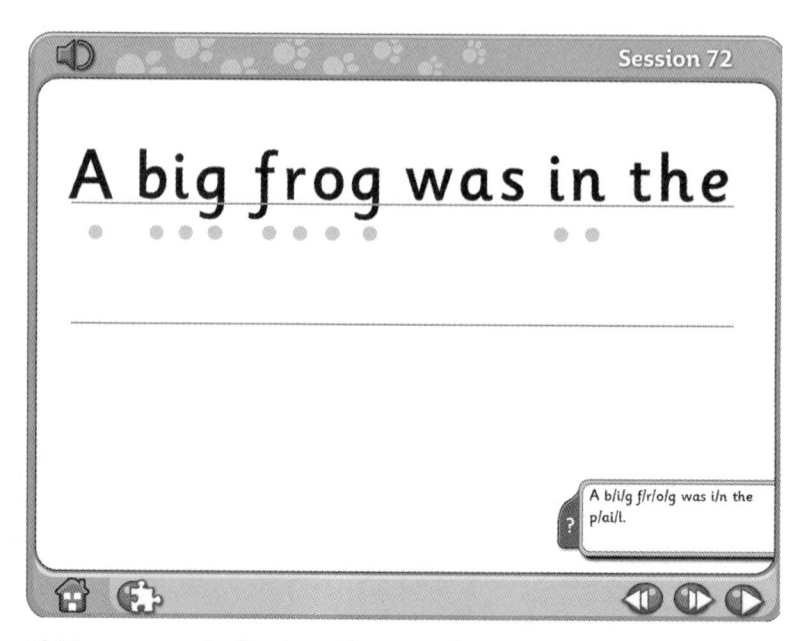

Children can see the forming of letters as the sentence is written.

Three support stages

Collins Big Cat Phonics gives three different levels of support, depending on the needs of the children. When children first learn new sounds, they have 100% support. When they are practising recently acquired sounds, they move to 50% support. When they have practised these sounds for some time, they are prompted to respond independently.

To change the default setting to provide additional practice for a group or individuals, go to the Teacher Support screen.

Stage 1 100% support

The first four sections – Say (phoneme acquisition), Blend (blending), Chop (segmenting) and Fast words (irregular words) – are modelled by the on-screen characters, Big Cat and Snappy, who prompt the children to **join in** with them. Children have 100% support when a new phoneme or fast word is introduced and for initial practising of blending and segmenting.

Example:
Big Cat says: *I say **c**. You say **c**.*

Stage 2 50% support

The first four sections are modelled by the characters. The characters prompt the children to repeat but they **do not join in** with the children as the children respond. This allows you to observe individual children or groups and to note their oral response, checking the knowledge and recall that children have of sounds, blending, segmenting, or recognition of fast words.

Example:
Big Cat says: *I say **c**. You say …*

Stage 3 Independent (0%) support

The first four sections run with **no help from the characters**. This allows you to observe individuals or groups and to note what the children have learnt and what they may need to practise.

Example:
The phoneme **c** appears. Children say it without any help from Big Cat.

Duplicate grapheme phonemes

At 0% support, phonemes that have more than one sound can appear in the same session, e.g. 'oo' as in 'look' and 'oo' as in 'moon'. Children can call out any of the different sounds as they are all correct, but you could take the opportunity to pause the session to discuss the differences.

Read and write sections

These sections run automatically with the characters voicing the building of the sentences. However, if you wish to remove the audio assistance, simply turn the sound off using the speaker icon on screen.

Collins Big Cat Phonics Readers

24 *Collins Big Cat Phonics Readers* have been written to help children apply the phonic knowledge and skills they have acquired using *Collins Big Cat Phonics*.

The readers are organised in four stages which correspond with the following guided reading bands: Stage 1 – Red A/Band 2A; Stage 2 – Red B/Band 2B; Stage 3 – Yellow/Band 3; Stage 4 – Blue/Band 4.

This guide provides book-by-book details and planning notes for all *Collins Big Cat Phonics* reading books.

Book band	About the book		Text type	Curriculum links
Red A / Band 2A	**Cat and Dog in a Mess** Shoo Rayner	A simple story about the lively characters Cat and Dog. When Cat and Dog play in the park, Dog gets into a mess. The character profiles on pages 14 and 15 help children compare and contrast Cat and Dog. This story is paired with the simple non-fiction recount about cats, *Pet Cat, Big Cat*.	A simple story with a familiar setting.	*Early Learning Goals:* *Physical development:* Recognise the importance of keeping healthy and the things that contribute towards this.
Red A / Band 2A	**Ant and Snail** Paul Shipton	A traditional story with alternative characters. Ant and Snail decide to have a race. Ant speeds off and is soon in the lead, but when Ant trips over and falls in a pit, he is glad when Snail arrives to help him. Children can follow and discuss the route taken by Ant and Snail using the map on pages 14 and 15.	A simple traditional story.	*Early Learning Goals:* *Creative development:* Explore colour, texture, shape, form and space in 2 and 3 dimensions.
Red A / Band 2A	**Muck It Up!** Jane Clarke	The two frogs in this simple story love to play in and around the pond. When Plip and Plop muck up the pond and reeds, they decide to clean it up. But Duck has other ideas. A story map on pages 14 and 15 allows children to recap the story.	A simple story with a familiar setting.	*Early Learning Goals:* *Personal and social development:* Have a developing awareness of their own needs, views and feelings and be sensitive to the needs, views and feelings of others *Knowledge and understanding of the world:* Find out about their environment and talk about those features they like and dislike. *Physical development:* Recognise the importance of keeping healthy and the things that contribute towards this.
Red A / Band 2A	**Pet Cat, Big Cat** Alison Hawes	A simple photographic recount that compares the behaviour of pet cats and big cats. Children can compare and contrast pet cats and big cats alongside each other on pages 14 and 15. This non-fiction book is paired with a story that features a cat: *Cat and Dog in a Mess* by Shoo Rayner.	A simple recount.	*Early Learning Goals:* *Knowledge and understanding of the world:* Find out about, and identify some features of, living things, objects and events they observe; look closely at similarities, differences, patterns and change.

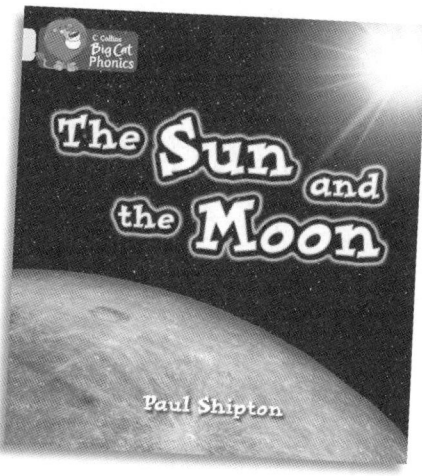

Learning objectives	**Focus phonemes**	**Fast word**
Early Learning Goals: *Communication, language and literacy:* Extend their vocabulary, exploring the meanings and sounds of new words; Hear and say sounds in words in the order in which they occur; Use their phonic knowledge to read simple regular words and make phonetically plausible attempts at more complex words. *Speaking, Listening and Learning objectives:* *ELG:* Use talk to organise, sequence and clarify thinking, feelings and events. *Scottish 5-14 Strands:* Listening, Talking, Reading, Writing, Level A.	t (cat, tub, let, cut, not) ck (pick, stuck, spick) e (mess, let) **Other new phonemes:** s, a, i, n, c, e, o, r, m, d, g, u, l, h, f, b	was, the, to
Early Learning Goals: *Communication, language and literacy:* Hear and say sounds in words in the order in which they occur; Extend vocabulary, exploring the meanings and sounds of new words; Use their phonic knowledge to read simple regular words and make phonetically plausible attempts at more complex words; Attempt writing for different purposes, using features of different forms such as lists, stories and instructions. *Speaking, Listening and Learning objectives:* *ELG:* Use talk to organise, sequence and clarify thinking, ideas, feelings, events. *Scottish 5-14 Strands:* Listening, Talking, Reading, Writing, Level A.	ai (snail), f (fit, fast), n (ant, snail, run, not, ran, in), r (run, ran, rock, rest) **Other new phonemes:** a, t, i, n, c, e, o, r, m, d, g, u, l, h, f, b	was, the, to, he
Early Learning Goals: *Communication, language and literacy:* Extend vocabulary, exploring the meanings and sounds of new words; Hear and say sounds in words in the order in which they occur. *Speaking, Listening and Learning objectives:* *ELG:* Use talk to organise, sequence and clarify thinking, ideas, feelings and events. *Scottish 5-14 Strands:* Listening, Talking, Reading, Writing, Level A.	u (muck, duck, fun, up), p (pond, mop), o (pond, Plop, not), m (muck, mess, mop) **Other new phonemes:** s, a, t, i, ck, e, r, d, g, u, l	the, is
Early Learning Goals: *Communication, language and literacy:* Extend vocabulary, exploring the meanings and sounds of new words; Hear and say sounds in words in the order in which they occur; Show understanding of how information can be found in non-fiction texts to answer questions about where, who, why and how; Use their phonic knowledge to make phonetically plausible attempts and more complex words. *Speaking, Listening and Learning objectives:* *ELG:* Use talk to organise, sequence and clarify thinking, ideas, feelings, events. *Scottish 5-14 Strands:* Listening, Talking, Reading, Writing, Level A.	i (sit, in, hiss), c (cat, cross), h (hunt, hiss), l (lap, lot) **Other new phonemes:** s, a, t, p, n, k, e, o, r, m, d, g, u, h, f, b	I, the

Book band	About the book	Text type	Curriculum links
Red A / Band 2A	**Run, Jump, Hop** *John Foster* This photographic non-fiction book examines how animals and people move. Each spread describes what a different animal can do, culminating in showing how a boy can move like other animals if he wants to. Pages 14 and 15 give children the opportunity to recap and discuss the text.	A simple non-fiction book.	*Early Learning Goals:* *Physical development:* Move with confidence, imagination and in safety.
Red A / Band 2A	**The Big Red Bus** *Alison Hawes* This simple non-fiction recount takes children on a trip with a little girl and her dad as they go for a journey on the big, red bus. They travel through the town and countryside to Nut Hill where the little girl meets her granddad. The story map on pages 14 and 15 gives children the opportunity to recap the text.	A simple recount.	*Early Learning Goals:* *Knowledge and understanding of the world:* Observe, find out about and identify features in the place they live and the natural world.
Red B / Band 2B	**The Mouse and the Monster** *Martin Waddell* A traditional retelling by Martin Waddell who tells the tale of how a mouse escapes the clutches of a hungry monster using his wits alone. Children can compare and contrast the two main characters using the character summaries on pages 14 and 15.	A traditional story.	*Early Learning Goals:* *Knowledge and understanding of the world:* Ask questions about why things happen and how things work; Look closely at similarities, differences, patterns and change.
Red B / Band 2B	**Bot on the Moon** *Shoo Rayner* A simple fantasy story in which Bot, the golf-loving robot, goes for a trip in his rocket ship. Bot buys a moon rock from the Moon Shop and begins to play golf, but disaster strikes when he lets go of his club. A story map on pages 14 and 15 lets children recap and discuss the story.	A simple fantasy story.	*Early Learning Goals:* *Creative development:* Use their imagination in art and design, music, dance, imaginative and role play and stories.
Red B / Band 2B	**We Are Not Fond of Rat!** *Emma Chichester Clark* A rhyming story about making friends. No one wants to be Rat's friend, but when the other animals see how sad he is, they all try to make him feel better. A story plan on pages 14 and 15 allows children the opportunity to recap and discuss the story. This story is paired with the non-fiction recount on a similar theme: *Feelings* by Monica Hughes.	A rhyming story.	*Early Learning Goals:* *Personal social and emotional development:* Respond to significant experiences, showing a range of feelings when appropriate; Have a developing awareness of their own needs, views and feelings and be sensitive to the needs, views and feelings of others.

Learning objectives	Focus phonemes	Fast words
Early Learning Goals: *Communication, language and literacy:* Hear and say sounds in words in the order in which they occur; Show understanding of how information can be found in non-fiction texts to answer questions about where, who, why and how; Use their phonic knowledge to make phonetically plausible attempts and more complex words; Extend vocabulary, exploring the meanings and sounds of new words. *Speaking, Listening and Learning objectives:* *ELG:* Use talk to organise, sequence and clarify thinking, ideas, feelings, events. *Scottish 5-14 Strands:* Listening, Talking, Reading, Writing, Level A.	j (jump), a (cat, can, fast), d (dog, dig, mud) **Other new phonemes:** s, t, i, p, n, c/k, e, o, r, g, u, l, h, f, b, ai	a, the, he
Early Learning Goals: *Communication, Language and Literacy:* Hear and say sounds in words in the order in which they occur; Show understanding of how information can be found in non-fiction texts to answer questions about where, who, why and how; Use their phonic knowledge to make phonetically plausible attempts and more complex words. *Speaking, Listening and Learning objectives* *ELG:* Use language to imagine and recreate roles and experiences. *Scottish 5-14 Strands:* Listening, Talking, Reading, Writing, Level A.	b (big, bus, back, bell) g (get, granddad), t (at, it, Nut, sit) **Other new phonemes:** s, a, i, p, n, c/k, e, o, r, d, u, l	the, to, a, we, of, I
Early Learning Goals: *Communication, Language and Literacy:* Extend vocabulary, exploring the meanings and sounds of new words; Hear and say sounds in words in the order in which they occur; Use their phonic knowledge to make phonetically plausible attempts at more complex words; Write things such as labels and captions and begin to form simple sentences, sometimes using punctuation. *Speaking, Listening and Learning objectives:* *ELG Communication language and literacy:* Use language to imagine and recreate roles and experiences. *Scottish 5-14 Strands:* Listening, Talking, Reading, Writing, Level A.	sh (bash, smash, crash), er (monster, bigger) oa (road), ng (looking, thinking, strong) **Other new phonemes:** ou, th (this), th (think), ee, w, oo (look), ie (pie), ch	the, was, said, I'm, you, of, to
Early Learning Goals: *Communication, Language and Literacy:* Extend vocabulary, exploring the meanings and sounds of new words; Hear and say sounds in words in the order in which they occur; Use their phonic knowledge to make phonetically plausible attempts at more complex words. *Speaking, Listening and Learning objectives:* *ELG Communication language and literacy:* Use talk to organise, sequence and clarify thinking. *Scottish 5-14 Strands:* Listening, Talking, Reading, Writing, Level A.	oo (moon, zoom), z (zoom), ar (stars, card) **Other new phonemes:** sh, ng, ou, ch	was, to, the, all, said, go, he, my, I
Early Learning Goals: *Communication, Language and Literacy:* hear and say sounds in words in the order in which they occur; Use their phonic knowledge to make phonetically plausible attempts at more complex words; Extend vocabulary, exploring the meanings and sounds of new words. *Speaking, Listening and Learning objectives:* *ELG Communication language and literacy:* Retell narratives in the correct sequence, drawing on language patterns of stories. *Scottish 5-14 Strands:* Listening, Talking, Reading, Writing, Level A.	qu (quack), th (them), ch (chat) **Other new phonemes:** sh, th (thin), ng, ee, z, w, oo (look), ie (lie), y	we, are, of, I, all, to, said, they, like, was

Book band	About the book	Text type	Curriculum links
Red B / Band 2B	**Pond Dipping** *Alison Hawes* *Pond Dipping* is a non-fiction recount of a boy and his mother exploring their local pond and the creatures that inhabit it. This non-fiction book supports work on nature and the world around you. The labelled illustration on pages 14 and 15 enables children to discuss what they have learned about pond life.	A simple non-fiction recount.	*Early Learning Goals:* *Personal, social and emotional development:* Understand what is right, what is wrong, and why. *Knowledge and understanding of the world:* Find out about, and identify some features of, living things, objects and events they observe; Observe, find out about, and identify features in the place they live and the natural world. *Creative development:* Explore colour, texture, shape, form and space in two and three dimensions.
Red B / Band 2B	**Feelings** *Monica Hughes* This gentle non-fiction book examines a range of feelings through the characters of a little boy and his dog. It encourages children to talk about their own feelings. Pages 14 and 15 offer children the opportunity to recap and discuss the boy's feelings. *Feelings* is paired with a story that shares the feeling theme: *We Are Not Fond of Rat!* by Emma Chichester Clark.	A simple non-fiction recount.	*Early Learning Goals:* *Personal, social and emotional development:* Understand what is right, what is wrong, and why; Consider the consequences of their words and actions for themselves and others.
Red B / Band 2B	**Thick and Thin** *Alison Hawes* A simple photographic non-fiction book contrasting thick and thin things. Children discover the qualities of different thick and thin materials and why children use them. Pages 14 and 15 give children the opportunity to recap and discuss the text.	A simple information book.	*Early Learning Goals:* *Knowledge and understanding of the world:* Investigate objects and materials by using all of their senses as appropriate. *Creative development:* Explore colour, texture, shape, form and space; *Physical development:* Handle tools, objects, construction and malleable materials with increasing control.
Yellow / Band 3	**Bart the Shark** *Paul Shipton* *Bart the Shark* is a humorous rhyming story about a shark who intimidates the smaller fish in the sea. Only the little pink crab isn't afraid of the big, greedy shark, for very obvious reasons! Use the labelled character profile on pages 14–15 to discuss Bart the Shark.	A humorous rhyming story.	Music: Sounds interesting – Exploring sounds; Citizenship: Choices.
Yellow / Band 3	**Horse Up a Tree** *Martin Waddell* *Horse Up a Tree* is a humorous story about a horse who went up a tree one day and didn't think about how to get down again. Use the table in the Farmer's handbook on pages 14–15 to discuss how the animals and the Farmer solved Horse's problem.	A humorous story.	Art and design: Picture this!

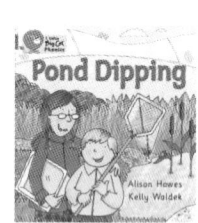

Learning objectives	Focus phonemes	Fast words
Early Learning Goals: *Communication, Language and Literacy:* Hear and say sounds in words in the order in which they occur; Use their phonic knowledge to make phonetically plausible attempts at more complex words; Extend vocabulary, exploring the meanings and sounds of new words; Show an understanding of how information can be found in non-fiction texts to answer questions about where, who, why and how. *Speaking, Listening and Learning objectives:* *ELG Communication language and literacy:* Use talk to organise, sequence and clarify thinking, ideas, feelings and events. *Scottish 5-14 Strands:* Listening, Talking, Reading, Writing, Level A.	x (box, six), w (wet, swim), ue (blue) **Other new phonemes:** ou, sh, th (them), ng, ee, oo (look)	I, are, a, the, my, of, we, all, into, like
Early Learning Goals: *Communication, Language and Literacy:* Hear and say sounds in words in the order in which they occur; Use their phonic knowledge to make phonetically plausible attempts at more complex words; Extend vocabulary, exploring the meanings and sounds of new words; Show an understanding of how information can be found in non-fiction texts to answer questions about where, who, why and how. *Speaking, Listening and Learning objectives:* *ELG Communication language and literacy:* Use talk to organise, sequence and clarify thinking, ideas, feelings and events. *Scottish 5-14 Strands:* Listening, Talking, Reading, Writing, Level A.	ou (shout, out), ee (feeling), ie (died, cried), or (torch) **Other new phonemes:** ar, er, ou, th (this), ng, w, oo (look), y	I, like, to, go, my, the, of, was, he, we, all
Early Learning Goals: *Communication, Language and Literacy:* Hear and say sounds in words in the order in which they occur; Use their phonic knowledge to make phonetically plausible attempts at more complex words; Extend vocabulary, exploring the meanings and sounds of new words; Attempt writing for different purposes, using features of different forms such as lists, stories and instructions. *Speaking, Listening and Learning objectives:* *ELG Communication language and literacy:* Use talk to organise, sequence and clarify thinking, ideas, feelings and events. *Scottish 5-14 Strands:* Listening, Talking, Reading, Writing, Level A.	th (thick, thin), oo (cook), v (names Bev, Kevin), oi (coil) **Other new phonemes:** ar, er, ou, sh, th (this), ee, z, oo (cool)	the, likes, of, he, she
NLS Framework Objectives Y1 T1 T2: Use phonological, contextual, grammatical and graphic knowledge to work out, predict and check the meanings of unfamiliar words and to make sense of what they read; T3 W1: Blend phonemes for reading. *Speaking, Listening and Learning objectives Y1* Drama 4: Explore familiar themes and characters through improvisation and role-play. *Scottish 5-14 Strands:* Listening, Talking, Reading, Writing, Level A.	a-e (cave, shape), ea (eat, seaweed), i-e (hide), y (hungry)	the, was, she, said, here, saw, have, we, who, he, a, very, are, some, to, does
NLS Framework Objectives Y1 T3 W1: Blend phonemes for reading; T1 W9: Read on sight approximately 30 high frequency words identified for Y1 and Y2; T1 T2: Use phonological, contextual, grammatical and graphic knowledge to work out, predict and check the meanings of unfamiliar words and to make sense of what they read; T1 T3: Use the language and features of non-fiction texts, e.g. labelled diagrams, captions for pictures, to make class books. *Speaking, Listening and Learning objectives Y1* Drama 4: Explore familiar themes and characters through improvisation and role-play. *Scottish 5-14 Strands:* Listening, Talking, Reading, Writing, Level A.	ay (day, hay, nay), ow (below, show), a-e (mane), o-e (broke)	the, to, they, all, what, said, some, one, do

Book band	About the book	Text type	Curriculum links
Yellow / Band 3	**Diggety Dog** *Michaela Morgan* *Diggety Dog* is a humorous rhyming story about a dog who is looking for a bone. As he digs, he uncovers many animal characters, but when he finally finds the bone, he gets a big surprise. The map of Diggety's hole on pages 14–15 allows children to discuss the characters the dog met along the way.	A humorous rhyming story.	Science: Plants and animals in the local environment
Yellow / Band 3	**Real Monsters** *Nic Bishop* *Real Monsters* takes children on a journey with a monster-like lizard, as it goes out looking for food. The summary on pages 14 and 15 allows children to recap on what happened in the text. *Real Monsters* is paired with the story *Bart the Shark* which is about fictional animals that live in the sea.	A non-fiction recount.	Science: Variation – grouping animals and plants
Yellow / Band 3	**Rock Out!** *Janice Vale* An action-packed photographic book that shows how a group of children make music with home-made instruments. *Rock Out!* explores the sound the instruments make and the rhythm of the music they make together. Use pages 14 and 15 to discuss the different home-made instruments used by the children in the book.	A non-fiction recount.	Music: Feel the pulse – Exploring pulse and rhythm; What's the score? – Exploring instruments and symbols; Science: Sound and hearing.
Yellow / Band 3	**The Sun and the Moon** *Paul Shipton* This simple non-fiction book introduces facts about the Sun and the Moon, and compares them. Use the fact files on pages 14 and 15 to compare and contrast the facts children have learned from the book.	A simple non-fiction book.	Maths: Use language such as 'circle' or 'bigger' to describe the shape and size of solids and flat shapes.
Blue / Band 4	**Mole and the New Hole** *Jane Clark* Mole is looking for a new hole to stay in, but he doesn't want to be on his own. In this simple story with a familiar setting, mole travels up the hill in search of an animal who will share their hole with him. Children can use the cross-section of the hill on pages 14 and 15 to discuss the characters and story setting.	A story with a familiar setting.	Citizenship: Choices; Science: Plants and animals in the local environment.

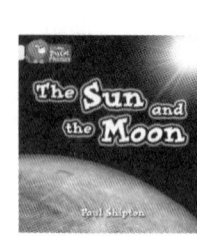

Learning objectives	Focus phonemes	Fast words
NLS Framework Objectives Y1 T2 W3: Blend phonemes in words with clusters for reading; T1 T2: Use phonological, contextual, grammatical and graphic knowledge to work out, predict and check the meanings of unfamiliar words and to make sense of what they read; T1 W9: Read on sight approximately 30 high frequency words identified for Y1 and Y2. *Speaking, Listening and Learning objectives Y1* Speaking 5: Retell stories, ordering events using story language. *Scottish 5-14 Strands:* Listening, Talking, Reading, Writing, Level A.	y (ugly, spotty, greedy, very, smelly, slithery, happy, sleepy, dizzy), o-e (bone, mole, vole, joke), ea (tea), i-e (time)	the, I, want, to, what, was, who, some, said, there, like(d), all, no, go
NLS Framework Objectives Y1 T3 W1: Blend phonemes for reading; T1 T2: Use phonological, contextual, grammatical and graphic knowledge to work out, predict and check the meanings of unfamiliar words and to make sense of what they read; T1 W9: Read on sight approximately 30 high frequency words identified for Y1 and Y2. *Speaking, Listening and Learning objectives Y1* Group discussion and interaction 7: Take turns to speak, listen to others' suggestions and talk about what they are going to do. *Scottish 5-14 Strands:* Listening, Talking, Reading, Writing, Level A.	ea (real, lean), ew (chew), a-e (snake, safe), ay (way, away)	what, the, here, there, onto, like, all, something
NLS Framework Objectives Y1 T1 T2: Use phonological knowledge to work out, predict and check the meanings of unfamiliar words and to make sense of what they read; T3 W1: Blend phonemes for reading. *Speaking, Listening and Learning objectives Y1* Group discussion and interaction 3: Ask and answer questions, make relevant contributions, offer suggestions and take turns. *Scottish 5-14 Strands:* Listening, Talking, Reading, Writing, Level A.	i-e (like, slides, wire), u-e (tube), ea (beat, squeaks, squeals), igh (right, might), ow (low, slow)	she, wants, the, of, two, some, into, he, they, their
NLS Framework Objectives Y1 T1 T2: Use phonological knowledge to work out, predict and check the meanings of unfamiliar words and to make sense of what they read; T3 W1: Blend phonemes for reading; T3 T19: Identify simple questions and use text to find answers. To locate parts of text that give particular information including labelled diagrams and charts; T2 T22: Write labels for drawings and diagrams, e.g. growing beans, parts of the body. *Speaking, Listening and Learning objectives Y1* Group discussion and interaction 3: Ask and answer questions, make relevant contributions, offer suggestions and take turns. *Scottish 5-14 Strands:* Listening, Talking, Reading, Writing, Level A.	igh (high, right, night, light), y (sky), ay (daytime, away), a-e (make, made, pale, same), i-e (shine), y (very, rocky).	the, to, all, you, do, some, because, there, no, come(s), they
NLS Framework Objectives Y1 T3 W1: Blend phonemes for reading; T1 T2: Use phonological, contextual, grammatical and graphic knowledge to work out, predict and check the meanings of unfamiliar words and to make sense of what they read; T1 T7: Re-enact stories in a variety of ways, e.g. through role-play. *Speaking, Listening and Learning objectives Y1* Speaking 1: Describe incidents or tell stories from their own experience, in an audible voice. *Scottish 5-14 Strands:* Listening, Talking, Reading, Writing, Level A.	are (share)	the, was, he, to, of, I, your, you, said, do, go, this, with, one, have, here, his, were, coming, is, a, we, come

Book band	About the book	Text type	Curriculum links
Blue / Band 4	**The Small Bun** *Martin Waddell* *The Small Bun* is a lively retelling of the traditional story *The Gingerbread Man*. A hungry man and his wife baked a small bun. But as soon as they put it on their plate, the bun jumped up and ran off. Use the story map on pages 14 and 15 to discuss the route the small bun took and the characters he met.	A traditional story.	Numeracy: Shape, space and measure
Blue / Band 4	**Hansel and Gretel** *Malachy Doyle* This is a simple retelling of the Grimm fairytale by Malachy Doyle. Hansel and Gretel are left alone in the wood and have to find their way home. Use the story map on pages 14 and 15 to discuss Hansel and Gretel's route home. This story is paired with a non-fiction book on a similar theme: *Birds*.	A traditional story.	Citizenship: Children's rights – human rights
Blue / Band 4	**The Rainforest at Night** *Nic Bishop* At night in the rainforest, things start to happen. Meet the animals and insects that live in the rainforest, in this simple non-fiction recount. A summary of the creatures that live in the rainforest can be found on pages 14 and 15.	An information book.	Art and design: Mother Nature, designer; Science: Light and dark
Blue / Band 4	**How to Grow a Beanstalk** *Janice Vale* This simple instruction text shows you how to take a bean and grow a beanstalk. The flow chart on page 14 and 15 give children the chance to recap and discuss the different stages of the process.	A simple instruction text.	Science: Growing plants
Blue / Band 4	**Birds** *Jilly MacLeod* From sea birds to woodland birds – this colourful photographic book introduces children to a wide variety of birds from around the world. The summary on pages 14 and 15 allows children to compare and contrast different types of birds. This non-fiction title is paired with a story with a similar theme: *Hansel and Gretel*.	A simple information book.	Science: Plants and animals; Variation.

Learning objectives	Focus phonemes	Fast words
NLS Framework Objectives Y1 T3 W1: Blend phonemes for reading; T1 W9: Read on sight approximately 30 high frequency words identified for Y1 and Y2; T1 T6: Recite stories and rhymes with predictable and repeating patterns, extemporising on patterns orally by substituting words and phrases, extending patterns, inventing patterns and playing with rhyme; T2 T22: Write labels for drawings and diagrams, e.g. growing beans, parts of the body. *Speaking, Listening and Learning objectives:* Speaking 5: Retell stories, ordering events using story language. *Scottish 5-14 Strands:* Listening, Talking, Reading, Writing, Level A.	al (small)	the, to, he, so, said, I, you, what, little, was, there, after, they, have, me, no
NLS Framework Objectives Y1 T3 W1: Blend phonemes for reading; T1 W9: Read on sight approximately 30 high frequency words identified for Y1 and Y2; T1 T2: Use phonological, contextual, grammatical and graphic knowledge to work out, predict and check the meanings of unfamiliar words and to make sense of what they read. *Speaking, Listening and Learning objectives Y1* Speaking 5: Retell stories, ordering events using story language. *Scottish 5-14 Strands:* Listening, Talking, Reading, Writing, Level A.	oy (boy), ir (birds, girl, dirt), au (cauldron), al (walk), aw (caw, saw), air (hair)	were, very, could, put
NLS Framework Objectives Y1 T1 W10: Learn new words from reading linked to particular topics, to build individual collections of personal interest or significant words; T3 W1: Blend phonemes for reading; T1 T2: Use phonological, contextual, grammatical and graphic knowledge to work out, predict and check the meanings of unfamiliar words and to make sense of what they read. *Speaking, Listening and Learning objectives Y1* Drama 4: Explore familiar themes and characters through improvisation and role-play. *Scottish 5-14 Strands:* Listening, Talking, Reading, Writing, Level A.	(crawl), al (talk, small), are (care)	the, when, to, a, they, little, their, come, some, away, have, so
NLS Framework Objectives Y1 T3 W1: Blend phonemes for reading; T1 T2: Use phonological, contextual, grammatical and graphic knowledge to work out, predict and check the meanings of unfamiliar words and to make sense of what they read. *Speaking, Listening and Learning objectives Y1* Group discussion and interaction 3: Ask and answer questions, make relevant contributions, offer suggestions and take turns. *Scottish 5-14 Strands:* Listening, Talking, Reading, Writing, Level A.	ur (curl, turning), al (beanstalk, small, tall), ow (how)	you, a, into, what, the, some, so, should, there, of, when, your
NLS Framework Objectives Y1 T3 W1: to blend phonemes for reading; T1 W9: to read on sight approximately 30 high frequency words identified for Y1 and Y2; T1 S1: to expect written text to make sense and to check for sense if it does not; T1 T2: Use phonological, contextual, grammatical and graphic knowledge to work out, predict and check the meanings of unfamiliar words and to make sense of what they read. *Speaking, Listening and Learning objectives Y1* Group discussion and interaction 7: Take turns to speak, listen to others' suggestions and talk about what they are going to do. *Scottish 5-14 Strands:* Listening, Talking, Reading, Writing, Level A.	ow (clown, towns, down), air (air), ir (birds), al (all, taller, small, talk, tall), aw (prawns, claws)	you, the, have, they, by, to, very, are, when, some, their, one

Collins Big Cat Phonics and learning objectives

This guide provides details of the *PNS Framework Objectives*, *Early Learning Goals* and *QCA Speaking, Listening and Learning objectives* addressed by each section of *Collins Big Cat Phonics*.

	Learning objectives	Speaking and listening
Say	**Early Learning Goals:** *Communication, Language and Literacy:* link sounds to letters, naming and sounding the letters of the alphabet. **PNS Framework Objectives:** YR W2: Knowledge of grapheme/phoneme correspondences through reading letters that represent the sounds a–z, ch, sh, th; YR W3: Alphabetic and phonic knowledge through sounding each letter of the alphabet; Y1 T2 W1: Secure identification, spelling and reading of letter sounds; Y1 T3 W1: The common spelling patterns for each of the long vowel phonemes: ee ai ie oa oo (long as in moon); identify phonemes in speech and writing.	Listening 2: Listen with sustained concentration; Group discussion and interaction 3: Ask and answer questions, make relevant contributions, offer suggestions and take turns; Listening 6: Listen and follow instructions accurately, asking for help and clarification if necessary.
Blend	**Early Learning Goals:** *Communication, Language and Literacy:* hear and say sounds in words in the order in which they occur; use phonic knowledge to read simple regular words and make phonetically plausible attempts at more complex words. **PNS Framework Objectives:** Y1 T1 W5: Blend phonemes to read CVC words in rhyming and non-rhyming sets; Y1 T2 W3: Blend phonemes in words with clusters for reading; Y1 T3 W1: Blend phonemes for reading.	Listening 2: Listen with sustained concentration; Group discussion and interaction 3: Ask and answer questions, make relevant contributions, offer suggestions and take turns; Listening 6: Listen and follow instructions accurately, asking for help and clarification if necessary.
Chop	**Early Learning Goals:** *Communication, Language and Literacy:* hear and say sounds in words in the order in which they occur; use phonic knowledge to write simple regular words and make phonetically plausible attempts at more complex words. **PNS Framework Objectives:** Y1 T1 W4: Discriminate and segment all three phonemes in CVC words; Y1 T2 W3: Segment clusters into phonemes for spelling; Y1 T3 W1: Segment words into phonemes for spelling.	Listening 2: Listen with sustained concentration; Group discussion and interaction 3: Ask and answer questions, make relevant contributions, offer suggestions and take turns; Listening 6: Listen and follow instructions accurately, asking for help and clarification if necessary.
Fast words	**Early Learning Goals:** *Communication, Language and Literacy:* read a range of familiar and common words. **PNS Framework Objectives:** YR W6: Read on sight the 45 high frequency words to be taught by the end of YR; Y1 T1 W9: Read on sight approximately 30 high frequency words identified for Y1 and Y2; Y1 T2 W6: Read on sight approximately 30 more high frequency words; Y1 T3 W4: Read on sight approximately 30 more high frequency words.	Listening 2: Listen with sustained concentration; Group discussion and interaction 3: Ask and answer questions, make relevant contributions, offer suggestions and take turns; Listening 6: Listen and follow instructions accurately, asking for help and clarification if necessary.
Read	**Early Learning Goals:** *Communication, Language and Literacy:* read a range of familiar and common words. Hear and say sounds in words in the order in which they occur; use phonic knowledge to read simple regular words and make phonetically plausible attempts at more complex words. **PNS Framework Objectives:** Y1 T2 W3: Blend phonemes in words with clusters for reading; Y1 T3 W1: Blend phonemes for reading; Y1 T1 T1: Reinforce and apply their word-level skills through shared and guided reading; Y1 T1 T2: Use phonological, contextual, grammatical and graphic knowledge to work out, predict and check the meanings of unfamiliar words and to make sense of what they read.	Group discussion and interaction 3: Ask and answer questions, make relevant contributions, offer suggestions and take turns; Listening 6: Listen and follow instructions accurately, asking for help and clarification if necessary; Group discussion and interaction 7: Take turns to speak, listen to others' suggestions and talk about what they are going to do; Speaking 9: Interpret a text by reading aloud with some variety in pace and emphasis.

COLLINS BIG CAT PHONICS AND LEARNING OBJECTIVES

	Learning objectives	**Speaking and listening**
Write	**Early Learning Goals:** *Communication, Language and Literacy:* Use phonic knowledge to write simple regular words and make phonetically plausible attempts at more complex words. **PNS Framework Objectives:** YR T11: Through shared writing: understand how writing is formed directionally, a word at a time; understand how letters are formed and used to spell words; apply knowledge of letter-sound correspondences in helping the teacher to scribe, and rereading what the class has written; Y1 T1 W4: Discriminate and segment all three phonemes in CVC words; Y1 T2 W3: Segment clusters into phonemes for spelling; Y1 T3 W1: Segment words into phonemes for spelling; Y1 T1 T12: Through shared and guided writing, apply phonological, graphic knowledge and sight vocabulary to spell words accurately.	Listening 2: Listen with sustained concentration; Group discussion and interaction 3: Ask and answer questions, make relevant contributions, offer suggestions and take turns; Listening 6: Listen and follow instructions accurately, asking for help and clarification if necessary; Group discussion and interaction 7: Take turns to speak, listen to others' suggestions and talk about what they are going to do.

This section gives details of the *PNS Framework Objectives*, *Early Learning Goals* and *QCA Speaking, Listening and Learning objectives* addressed by the activities in *Collins Big Cat Phonics*.

	Learning objectives	**Speaking and listening**
Alphabet Song *Letter Shapes*	**Early Learning Goals:** *Communication, language and literacy:* link sounds to letters, naming and sounding the letters of the alphabet. **PNS Framework Objectives:** YR W3: Alphabetic and phonic knowledge through; • sounding and naming each letter of the alphabet in lower and upper case; • writing letters in response to letter names; • understanding alphabetical order through alphabet books, rhymes, and songs.	Listening 2: Listen with sustained concentration.
Hide and Seek *Jack and the Beanstalk*	**Early Learning Goals:** *Communication, Language and Literacy:* hear and say sounds in words in the order in which they occur; use their phonic knowledge to read simple regular words and make phonetically plausible attempts at more complex words. **PNS Framework Objectives:** Y1 T1 W5: Blend phonemes to read CVC words in rhyming and non-rhyming sets; Y1 T2 W3: Blend phonemes in words with clusters for reading; Y1 T3 W1: Blend phonemes for reading.	Group discussion and interaction 3: Ask and answer questions, make relevant contributions, offer suggestions and take turns; Listening 6: Listen and follow instructions accurately, asking for help and clarification if necessary.
Bubbles *Rainbow Letters*	**Early Learning Goals:** *Communication, Language and Literacy:* hear and say sounds in words in the order in which they occur; use their phonic knowledge to write simple regular words and make phonetically plausible attempts at more complex words. **PNS Framework Objectives:** Y1 T1 W4: Discriminate and segment all three phonemes in CVC words; Y1 T2 W3: Segment clusters into phonemes for spelling; Y1 T3 W1: Segment words into phonemes for spelling.	Group discussion and interaction 3: Ask and answer questions, make relevant contributions, offer suggestions and take turns; Listening 6: Listen and follow instructions accurately, asking for help and clarification if necessary.
Treasure Island	**Early Learning Goals:** *Communication, Language and Literacy:* read a range of familiar and common words. Hear and say sounds in words in the order in which they occur; use their phonic knowledge to read simple regular words and make phonetically plausible attempts at more complex words. **PNS Framework Objectives:** YR W6: Read on sight the 45 high frequency words to be taught by the end of YR; Y1 T1 W9: Read on sight approximately 30 high frequency words identified for Y1 and Y2; Y1 T2 W6: Read on sight approximately 30 more high frequency words; Y1 T3 W4: Read on sight approximately 30 more high frequency words; Y1 T1 W5: Blend phonemes to read CVC words in rhyming and non-rhyming sets; Y1 T2 W3: Blend phonemes in words with clusters for reading; Y1 T3 W1: Blend phonemes for reading.	Group discussion and interaction 3: Ask and answer questions, make relevant contributions, offer suggestions and take turns; Listening 6: Listen and follow instructions accurately, asking for help and clarification if necessary.

Collins Big Cat Phonics and the Scottish 5-14 Guidelines

The carefully planned systematic approach in *Collins Big Cat Phonics* supports the teaching of reading and writing as well as developing listening and talking skills through a daily 10-minute phonics session, using an electronic whiteboard or PC. It helps to:

- enrich children's spoken language
- develop a more extensive vocabulary
- encourage children to have a go at writing
- develop letter knowledge
- teach spelling at the same time as reading.

5-14 Strands: Attainment Targets	Sessions 1-6	7-26	27-46	47-66	67-86	87-106	107-126	127-146
Listening 1, Level A: For instructions and directions	✓	✓	✓	✓	✓	✓	✓	✓
Listening 5, Level A: Knowledge about language								
Talking 4, Level A: About texts				✓	✓	✓	✓	✓
Reading 1, Level A: For information		✓	✓	✓	✓	✓	✓	✓
Reading 2, Level A: For enjoyment		✓	✓	✓	✓	✓	✓	✓
Reading 4, Level A: Awareness of genre						✓	✓	✓
Reading 5, Level A: Aloud		✓	✓	✓	✓	✓	✓	✓
Reading 6, Level A: Knowledge about language								
Writing 1, Level A: Functional		✓	✓	✓	✓	✓	✓	✓
Writing 2, Level A: Personal					✓	✓	✓	✓
Writing 3, Level A: Imaginative				✓	✓	✓	✓	✓
Writing 4, Level A: Punctuation and structure		✓	✓	✓	✓	✓	✓	✓
Writing 5, Level A: Spelling		✓	✓	✓	✓	✓	✓	✓
Writing 6, Level A: Handwriting and presentation				✓	✓	✓	✓	✓

Collins Big Cat Phonics is designed for children starting the reading and writing process in P1 at level A and continuing in P2 at the beginning of level B. Not all children will be ready to start the full programme and some will take longer to work at an independent level. Teachers should therefore use the support provided on pages 57–76 to observe and assess children's readiness and progress.

147–166	167–186	187–196	197–206	207–216	217–226	227–236	237–246	247–256	257–266	267–276	277–286	287–299
✓	✓	✓	✓	✓	✓	✓	✓	✓	✓	✓	✓	✓
									✓	✓	✓	✓
✓	✓	✓	✓	✓	✓	✓	✓	✓	✓	✓	✓	✓
✓	✓	✓	✓	✓	✓	✓	✓	✓	✓	✓	✓	✓
✓	✓	✓	✓	✓	✓	✓	✓	✓	✓	✓	✓	✓
✓	✓	✓	✓	✓	✓	✓	✓	✓	✓	✓	✓	✓
✓	✓	✓	✓	✓	✓	✓	✓	✓	✓	✓	✓	✓
									✓	✓	✓	✓
✓	✓	✓	✓	✓	✓	✓	✓	✓	✓	✓	✓	✓
✓	✓	✓	✓	✓	✓	✓	✓	✓	✓	✓	✓	✓
✓	✓	✓	✓	✓	✓	✓	✓	✓	✓	✓	✓	✓
✓	✓	✓	✓	✓	✓	✓	✓	✓	✓	✓	✓	✓
✓	✓	✓	✓	✓	✓	✓	✓	✓	✓	✓	✓	✓
✓	✓	✓	✓	✓	✓	✓	✓	✓	✓	✓	✓	✓

Detailed programme outline

Collins Big Cat Phonics consists of 300 daily sessions, which build up to last approximately 10 minutes each. It is designed to be used with children aged 4–6 when they start school. Each session provides three stages of supported learning and practice.

Order and content of sessions

The following pages detail the order and content of all the sessions in *Collins Big Cat Phonics*. Each section – Say, Blend, Chop, Fast words, and Read or Write – is summarised so that you can see, at a glance, when new elements are introduced. The first time phonemes, words and sentences are introduced they appear in **bold**. You can also find practical tips about how to extend learning, using activities.

Sessions 1–6 (approximately 3–5 seconds)

Big Cat introduces the first six phonemes at the rate of one per day.

These daily sessions introduce the 'modelling' teaching principle: *I say… You say…*

Each session will be very short – by session 6, the whole session will only last 15 seconds!

1. Say	s a t i p n

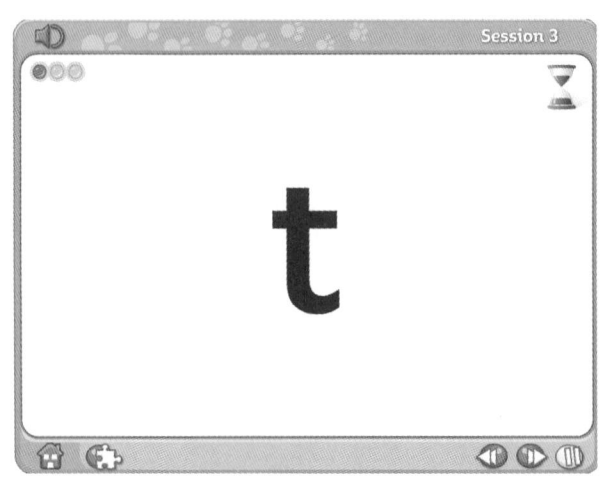

"I say 't'. You say 't'."

Sessions 7–26 (approximately 6 minutes)

These daily sessions introduce the 'repetition and practice' teaching principle by repeating previously learnt phonemes, initially in a fixed order, changing to a random order by session 21.

The first group of words for blending and segmenting and sentences are also introduced.

Fast (or irregular) words are introduced at session 20.

Tips

- Let the children see you joining in. Exaggerate your mouth and lip shapes!
- For blending, point to each sound, then sweep along the word to blend.
- For segmenting use finger counting with the children – signal each sound by raising a finger, starting with your thumb. If you are left-handed, start with the little finger of your left hand.
- Some children may find the session too long – you can stop at segmenting and return to fast words and Read/Write later in the day.
- Try the independent level to assess children's progress.
- Use Benchmark Assessment A to identify children who are making slower progress.

1. Say	**New phoneme introduced every day:** s a t i p n **c k ck e o r m d g u l h f b ai j oa ee z w oo** (as in *wood*) **oo** (as in *cool*) **ie**
2. Blend *Practised for 20 sessions*	Focus phoneme group for words: s a t i p n – sat tin pan tap ant sit pin pat nip snap
3. Chop *Practised for 20 sessions*	Focus phoneme group for words: s a t i p n – sat tin pan tap ant sit pin pat nip snap
4. Fast words *These start at session 20 and are added at the rate of two every five sessions*	I the • to was
5. Read or **Write** *Alternate sessions*	It is a tin.　　　　It is Nip. It is a pan.　　　Nip is in a pan. It is a tap.　　　Nip is in a tin. It is a pin.　　　Pat is in a tin. It is an ant.　　　Snap, snap, Pat!

Benchmark Assessment A (see page 63)

Sessions 27–46 (no longer than 10 minutes, for all subsequent sessions)

Tips

- For blending, point to each sound, then sweep along the word to blend.

- For segmenting use finger counting with the children – signal each sound by raising a finger, starting with your thumb. If you are left-handed, start with the little finger of your left hand.

- Play games using a 'robot' voice and a puppet who cannot blend three sounds. Say 't-a-p' and ask them which word it makes.

- Your observations of the children should indicate several children who will be ready for reading *Collins Big Cat Phonics Readers* Red A. Work with a small group of two to four children and see how they get on.

- Ask your teaching assistant to observe individual children that may be struggling, using Observation A on page 72 or Benchmark Assessment A on page 63. Is there a hearing difficulty?

1. Say *All phonemes from the first set have now been introduced. These go on being repeated every session until 150.*	s a t i p n c k ck e o r m d g u l h f b ai j oa ee z w oo (as in *wood*) oo (as in *cool*) ie **v y** (as in *yak*) **ch sh th** (as in *that*) **th** (as in *thank*) **ng x qu ar er ou oi u-e or**
2. Blend *Practised for 20 sessions*	Focus phoneme groups for words: s a t i p n • **c k ck e o r** – **can cat ran pop pet pen top rock stop nest**
3. Chop *Practised for 20 sessions*	Focus phoneme group for words: s a t i p n • **c k ck e o r** – **can cat ran pop pet pen top rock stop nest**
4. Fast words	I the • to was **he she • we said • you are • all they**
5. Read or **Write** *Alternate sessions*	It is a nest. It is a nest on a rock. Pop is a pet. Pop is a pet in a nest. Pop is on the top.	I am a rat. I am on the rock. I am on top. I am in the nest. Pop was in the nest. Stop, Pop!

Sessions 47–66

Tips

- Try out more children with *Collins Big Cat Phonics Readers*.

- Sing the *Alphabet Song* and do the *Rainbow Letters* activity on the CD-ROM. Do the *air-writing* activity. Using the outside learning area, ask the children to paint their names in water and to make an alphabet snake with letters.

- Make a duplicate set of name cards for sorting into sets, e.g. same initial letter, same number of syllables, boys' names, girls' names.

- Make up a story about Stan the slug.

- Break up the sessions by using an activity on the CD-ROM on one or two days.

- Praise children for writing as part of their play, e.g. in their role-play, they can write labels for the 'shop'.

- Praise children for attempting to spell words, using their phonic knowledge. Tell them Big Cat and Snappy would be pleased!

1. Say	s a t i p n c k ck e o r m d g u l h f b ai j oa ee z w oo (as in *wood*) oo (as in *cool*) ie v y (as in *yak*) ch sh th (as in *that*) th (as in *thank*) ng x qu ar er ou oi u-e or
2. Blend	Focus phoneme groups for words: s a t i p n • c k ck e o r • m d g u l – **dog get dig Mum Dad mess sun duck muck pond land slug Stan**
3. Chop	Focus phoneme groups for words: s a t i p n • c k ck e o r • m d g u l – **dog get dig Mum Dad mess sun duck muck pond land slug Stan**
4. Fast words	I the • to was • he she • we said • you are • all they **my come • me go • like no • have be**
5. Read or **Write** *Alternate sessions*	**Stan is a slug.** **The dog can get Stan.** **Stan was on the land.** **The duck was in the pond.** **The sun is on Mum and Dad.** **The pond is a mess.** **A duck is in the muck.** **Mum can get the dog.** **We said it was a mess.** **Mum can dig the land.**

The reading section in session 59

Sessions 67–86

Tips

- Focus on one group for spelling, a different group for blending, and so on. Ask the rest of the children to say words in their heads.
- Play the *Hide and Seek* and *Treasure Island* activities on the CD-ROM.
- Air-write letter names and shapes.
- Take the children for a print walk around the classroom. Ask them to spot letter sounds and letter names and say them. Ask them to write some signs, or write some with the children.
- Work one-to-one with children on their writing, sounding out words for them, scribing for them, making personal books using their own photographs and so on.
- Use stories to stimulate writing.
- Assess struggling children using Benchmark Assessment B on page 64. Is there a possible hearing or eyesight difficulty?
- For children who are progressing quickly, try the whole session at independent level.

1. Say	s a t i p n c k ck e o r m d g u l h f b ai j oa ee z w oo (as in *wood*) oo (as in *cool*) ie v y (as in *yak*) ch sh th (as in *that*) th (as in *thank*) ng x qu ar er ou oi u-e or
2. Blend	Focus phoneme groups for words: s a t i p n • ck ck e o r • m d g u l • **h f b ai j – bad bat fat jet had fill puff rain pail frost frog crab snail grab Spain**
3. Chop	Focus phoneme groups for words: s a t i p n • ck ck e o r • m d g u l • **h f b ai j – bad bat fat jet had fill puff rain pail frost frog crab snail grab Spain**
4. Fast words *All words from the first set have now been introduced, these go on being repeated every session.*	I the • to was • he she • we said • you are • all they • my come • me go • like no • have be **by one • so some**
5. Read or **Write** *Alternate sessions*	The fat bat is bad. A big frog was in the pail. The big frog can puff. Frost was on the grass. We can fill the pail. We had rain and sun in Spain. The crab can grab the pail. The big bat has fun. You are in Spain. Stan and the bat had a jet!

Benchmark Assessment B (see page 64)

DETAILED PROGRAMME OUTLINE

Sessions 87–106

Tips

- Praise any experimenting with phonemes in their writing. Tell them Big Cat and Snappy would be very pleased!
- Do the same for fast words they are writing.
- Practise saying **letter names** across fast words, e.g. t-h-e = the; w-a-s = was. This really helps spelling.
- Do 'fast' writing of these words on a small whiteboard.
- Play the *Hide and Seek* and *Treasure Island* activities on the CD-ROM. Air-write letter names and shapes.
- Model the writing of a letter – and get them to write thank-you letters to someone.
- Ask the children to try spelling some words from the sentences on small whiteboards.
- Use an activity on the CD-ROM in addition to some sessions, e.g. *Alphabet Song*, *Treasure Island*.
- Offer magnetic letters and a timer. Challenge them to make words quickly.

A fast word. Some everyday words are irregular or hard to decode.

1. Say	s a t i p n c k ck e o r m d g u l h f b ai j oa ee z w oo (as in *wood*) oo (as in *cool*) ie v y (as in *yak*) ch sh th (as in *that*) th (as in *thank*) ng x qu ar er ou oi u-e or
2. Blend	Focus phoneme groups for words: s a t i p n • c k ck e o r • m d g u l • h f b ai j • **oa ee z w oo** (as in *wood*) – **bee Zap weed feel buzz look goat toad jeep wood went toast sleep stood zebra**
3. Chop	Focus phoneme groups for words: s a t i p n • c k ck e o r • m d g u l • h f b ai j • **oa ee z w oo** (as in *wood*) – **bee Zap weed feel buzz look goat toad jeep wood went toast sleep stood zebra**
4. Fast words	I the • to was • he she • we said • you are • all they • my come • me go • like no • have be • by one • so some
5. Read or Write	Buzz went the bee. Zap fell on the toast. The jeep went fast. They are all in the jeep. Zap was not in my jeep. / Zap had his feet in the weed. A zebra was asleep. Look at the big zebra. I fell asleep in the wood. The goat and the toad feel good.

Sessions 107–126

Tips

- Alternate the reading of the words in the Read section by asking different children or a group to read.
- Play the *Letter Shapes* and *Bubbles* activities on the CD-ROM. Sky-write letter names and shapes.
- Write a story about Zap.
- Ask children to try spelling the words in the Write section, on small whiteboards.
- Use stories to stimulate writing.
- Draw around a child and fix the outline to the wall. Use this outline for Jack, from *Jack and the Beanstalk*.
- Ask them to write messages on labels and stick them in the outline.
- Identify children who would benefit from extra practice in small groups – use the support activities suggested in the Next steps section of the benchmark assessments on pages 61–62.
- Select *Collins Big Cat Phonics Readers* as appropriate for guided reading and use some follow-up activities based on the stories.

1. Say	s a t i p n c k ck e o r m d g u l h f b ai j oa ee z w oo (as in *wood*) oo (as in *cool*) ie v y (as in *yak*) ch sh th (as in *that*) th (as in *thank*) ng x qu ar er ou oi u-e or
2. Blend	Focus phoneme groups for words: s a t i p n • ck ck e o r • m d g u l • h f b ai j • oa ee z w oo (as in *wood*) • **oo** (as in *cool*) **ie v y** (as in *yak*) **ch** – **lie pie van vet yak moon pool rich vest chimp fries spoon**
3. Chop	Focus phoneme groups for words: s a t i p n • ck ck e o r • m d g u l • h f b ai j • oa ee z w oo (as in *wood*) • **oo** (as in *cool*) **ie v y** (as in *yak*) **ch** – **lie pie van vet yak moon pool rich vest chimp fries spoon**
4. Fast words	I the • to was • he she • we said • you are • all they • my come • me go • like no • have be • by one • so some
5. Read or **Write** *Alternate sessions*	I see one big pie. My rich vet was in a black van. The doll can lie in my bed. My yak can run fast. The vet in the van got the yak. I like to chat to my mum. The chimp sleeps in the green grass. She can see the moon in the pool. We like pie and fries. My spoon is in the pie.

DETAILED PROGRAMME OUTLINE

Sessions 127–146

Tips

- Work with individual children to write a letter to Big Cat or Snappy.
- Identify children who are finding ccvc words more difficult.
- Play the *Jack and the Beanstalk* and *Bubbles* activities on the CD-ROM.
- Sky-write letter names and shapes.
- Make an alphabet A–Z using packaging from food tins, snacks, cereal boxes, and so on.
- Model different types of writing.
- Make up a story about the vet and the chimp.
- Plan for children who are becoming fluent to read *Collins Big Cat Phonics Readers* again, choosing those they have particularly enjoyed.
- Some children will be ready to move on to Yellow or Blue *Collins Big Cat Phonics Readers*.
- Encourage children to use letter names when spelling fast words in their writing. Re-assess those children who are making little progress – is it a hearing, eyesight, behaviour or another learning difficulty?

1. Say	s a t i p n c k ck e o r m d g u l h f b ai j oa ee z w oo (as in *wood*) oo (as in *cool*) ie v y (as in *yak*) ch sh th (as in *that*) th (as in *thank*) ng x qu ar er ou oi u-e or
2. Blend	Focus phoneme groups for words: s a t i p n • c k ck e o r • m d g u l • h f b ai j • oa ee z w oo (as in *wood*) • oo (as in *cool*) ie v y (as in *yak*) ch • **sh th** (as in *that*) **th** (as in *thank*) **ng x** – **ox box fix fox bash fish dish thin teeth them ship sank thank swung brush**
3. Chop	Focus phoneme groups for words: s a t i p n • c k ck e o r • m d g u l • h f b ai j • oa ee z w oo (as in *wood*) • oo (as in *cool*) ie v y (as in *yak*) ch • **sh th** (as in *that*) **th** (as in *thank*) **ng x** – **ox box fix fox bash fish dish thin teeth them ship sank thank swung brush**
4. Fast words	I the • to was • he she • we said • you are • all they • my come • me go • like no • have be • by one • so some
5. Read or **Write** *Alternate sessions*	Max sat in the box. Max can bash the box. One big ox sat on the box. They can fix fish in the dish. The thin king had six teeth. I can see them by the ship. Max swung his brush. Thank the thin king. The fox had a fish in his teeth. The ship sank in the sea.

Sessions 147–166

At session 150 new phonemes and fast (or irregular) words are introduced.

Tips

- Some children will be ready to move on to Yellow or Blue *Collins Big Cat Phonics Readers*.
- Model the writing of your own sentences, linked to another area of learning.
- Ask the children to think of another sentence with different words, using the focus group of phonemes.
- Provide little blank books to make catalogues by sticking in pictures and writing the name and price of the items.
- Use the *Collins Big Cat Phonics Readers* and try some follow-up activities based on the stories – ideas are in the back of each book.
- Plan for children who are becoming fluent to read *Collins Big Cat Phonics Readers* again, choosing those they have particularly enjoyed.
- Encourage children to use letter names when spelling fast words in their writing.

1. Say	s a t i p n c k ck e o r m d g u l h f b ai j oa ee z w oo (as in *wood*) oo (as in *cool*) ie v y (as in *yak*) ch sh th (as in *that*) th (as in *thank*) ng x qu ar er ou oi u-e or **ay a-e ea y** (as in *sunny*) **igh i-e y** (as in *fly*) **ow** (as in *snow*) **o-e ew u-e ir ur au aw al oy**
2. Blend	Focus phoneme groups for words: s a t i p n • ck ck e o r • m d g u l • h f b ai j • oa ee z w oo (as in *wood*) • oo (as in *cool*) ie v y (as in *yak*) ch • sh th (as in *that*) th (as in *thank*) ng x • **qu ar er ou oi – car her star oil out charm dark coin queen count found point smart spoil smarter**
3. Chop	Focus phoneme groups for words: s a t i p n • ck ck e o r • m d g u l • h f b ai j • oa ee z w oo (as in *wood*) • oo (as in *cool*) ie v y (as in *yak*) ch • sh th (as in *that*) th (as in *thank*) ng x • **qu ar er ou oi – car her star oil out charm dark coin queen count found point smart spoil smarter**
4. Fast words *3 words every five sessions are added from session 150.*	I the • to was • he she • we said • you are • all they • my come • me go • like no • have be • by one • so some **little do her • did here there • saw when who • what where after**
5. Read or Write *Alternate sessions*	Look at my red car. My car needs oil. The queen was charming. Count up to ten. Point to the big star. Lots of oil ran from the car. The queen is in the black car. My red car is smarter than his. I found a coin by the dark green shed. Her star was the best one.

DETAILED PROGRAMME OUTLINE

Sessions 167–186

Tips

- Some children will be ready to move on to Yellow or Blue *Collins Big Cat Phonics Readers*.
- Encourage children to use letter names when spelling fast words in their writing.
- Play the *Treasure Island* activity on the CD-ROM. Sky-write letter names and shapes.
- Try a whole session at independent level.
- Use drama and stories to stimulate writing.
- Model different types of writing.
- Assess again those children who are struggling. What progress have they made since last time? Which 'next steps' suggestions worked?
- Try Benchmark Assessment C on page 65 if they have made good progress.

1. Say *All phonemes from the second set have now been introduced. These go on being repeated every session until 299.*	s a t i p n c k ck e o r m d g u l h f b ai j oa ee z w oo (as in *wood*) oo (as in *cool*) ie v y (as in *yak*) ch sh th (as in *that*) th (as in *thank*) ng x qu ar er ou oi u-e or ay a-e ea y (as in *sunny*) igh i-e y (as in *fly*) ow (as in *snow*) o-e ew u-e ir ur au aw al oy **ow** (as in *cow*) **air are**
2. Blend	Focus phoneme groups for words: s a t i p n • c k ck e o r • m d g u l • h f b ai j • oa ee z w oo (as in *wood*) • oo (as in *cool*) ie v y (as in *yak*) ch • sh th (as in *that*) th (as in *thank*) ng x • qu ar er ou oi • **ue or – for born corn fork torch torn glue blue storm stork shorter**
3. Chop	Focus phoneme groups for words: s a t i p n • c k ck e o r • m d g u l • h f b ai j • oa ee z w oo (as in *wood*) • oo (as in *cool*) ie v y (as in *yak*) ch • sh th (as in *that*) th (as in *thank*) ng x • qu ar er ou oi • **ue or – for born corn fork torch torn glue blue storm stork shorter**
4. Fast words	I the • to was • he she • we said • you are • all they • my come • me go • like no • have be • by one • so some • little do her • did here there • saw when who • what where after **because want were • your two very • don't people many • more could should**
5. Read or **Write** *Alternate sessions*	I like my blue torch. My torch is good in the dark. My comic was torn into bits. We like sweetcorn a lot. Storks have big wings. I was born in March. Storks sit in big nests at the top of trees. Storms can smash up sheds. Glue is good for mending things. My dad is shorter than my mum.

Benchmark Assessment C (see page 65)

Sessions 187–196

As children will now be more skilled in blending and segmenting, they will practise each set of focus phoneme groups for 10 sessions rather than 20.

As children will now be more skilled in reading and writing, the sentences are no longer the same.

Tips

- Some children will be ready to move on to Yellow or Blue *Collins Big Cat Phonics Readers*.
- Encourage children to use letter names when spelling out fast words in their writing.
- Ask the children to think of another sentence with different words, using the focus group of phonemes.
- Use drama and stories to stimulate writing.
- Use *Collins Big Cat Phonics Readers* and try some follow-up activities based on the stories – ideas are in the back of each book.
- Model different types of writing.
- Make up your own sentences for dictation activities using the focus phonemes.
- Ask more able writers to make up silly sentences for dictation, using the focus phonemes.

1. Say	s a t i p n c k ck e o r m d g u l h f b ai j oa ee z w oo (as in *wood*) oo (as in *cool*) ie v y (as in *yak*) ch sh th (as in *that*) th (as in *thank*) ng x qu ar er ou oi u-e or ay a-e ea y (as in *sunny*) igh i-e y (as in *fly*) ow (as in *snow*) o-e ew u-e ir ur au aw al oy ow (as in *cow*) air are
2. Blend	Focus phoneme groups for words: s a t i p n • ck ck e o r • m d g u l • h f b ai j • oa ee z w oo (as in *wood*) • oo (as in *cool*) ie v y (as in *yak*) ch • sh th (as in *that*) th (as in *thank*) ng x • qu ar er ou oi • ue or • **ay a-e – day way pay may cake game name made make shake play stay plane spade wave**
3. Chop	Focus phoneme groups for words: s a t i p n • ck ck e o r • m d g u l • h f b ai j • oa ee z w oo (as in *wood*) • oo (as in *cool*) ie v y (as in *yak*) ch • sh th (as in *that*) th (as in *thank*) ng x • qu ar er ou oi • ue or • **ay a-e – day way pay may cake game name made make shake play stay plane spade wave**
4. Fast words	I the • to was • he she • we said • you are • all they • my come • me go • like no • have be • by one • so some • little do her • did here there • saw when who • what where after • because want were • your two very • don't people many • more could should • **would put brother • down love their**

5. Read Reading sentences	5. Write Writing sentences
May I play with you? Waves come and go all day long. Stay with me and play until it is dark. She dug in the soil with a big spade. I had to pay for my game of golf.	They made milk shakes and drank them. We must pay for the lemon cake with my name on it. We like to play in the waves in summer. May I fly my plane in the garden? Stay and make pink cakes for Mum and Dad.

DETAILED PROGRAMME OUTLINE

Sessions 197–206

Tips

- Use drama and stories to stimulate writing.
- Use *Collins Big Cat Phonics Readers* and try some follow-up activities based on the stories – ideas are in the back of each book.
- Make up your own sentences for dictation activities using the focus phonemes.
- Challenge children to extend the sentence in some way.
- Ask more able writers to make up silly sentences for dictation, using the focus phonemes – like the sea being made of jelly!
- Plan for children who are becoming fluent to read the *Collins Big Cat Phonics Readers* again, choosing those they have particularly enjoyed.

1. Say	s a t i p n c k ck e o r m d g u l h f b ai j oa ee z w oo (as in *wood*) oo (as in *cool*) ie v y (as in *yak*) ch sh th (as in *that*) th (as in *thank*) ng x qu ar er ou oi u-e or ay a-e ea y (as in *sunny*) igh i-e y (as in *fly*) ow (as in *snow*) o-e ew u-e ir ur au aw al oy ow (as in *cow*) air are
2. Blend	Focus phoneme groups for words: s a t i p n • c k ck e o r • m d g u l • h f b ai j • oa ee z w oo (as in *wood*) • oo (as in *cool*) ie v y (as in *yak*) ch • sh th (as in *that*) th (as in *thank*) ng x • qu ar er ou oi • ue or • **ea y** (as in *sunny*) – **tea sea read peach beach teach clean dream sneak treat jelly sunny carry messy**
3. Chop	Focus phoneme groups for words: s a t i p n • c k ck e o r • m d g u l • h f b ai j • oa ee z w oo (as in *wood*) • oo (as in *cool*) ie v y (as in *yak*) ch • sh th (as in *that*) th (as in *thank*) ng x • qu ar er ou oi • ue or • **ea y** (as in *sunny*) – **tea sea read peach beach teach clean dream sneak treat jelly sunny carry messy**
4. Fast words *These have now all been added and continue being repeated.*	I the • to was • he she • we said • you are • all they • my come • me go • like no • have be • by one • so some • little do her • did here there • saw when who • what where after • because want were • your two very • don't people many • more could should • would put brother • down love their • **every likes**

5. Read Reading sentences

I drank a cup of tea in the sea!
On sunny days I go to the beach and play.
Mum made a peach jelly for my sister.
All my mates like fish and chips.
I can sneak a look at the green sports car.

5. Write Writing sentences

I had a dream that the sea was made of jelly.
Dad and Mum read good books on the beach.
One duck had messy wings from oil on the beach.
Fish and chips are a big treat for me.
Will you carry my peach for me?

Sessions 207–216

Tips

- Ask the children to think of another sentence with different words, using the focus group of phonemes.
- Use drama and stories to stimulate writing.
- Plan writing linked to your role-play area, e.g. labels for the 'garden centre' or for fruit in the 'shop'.
- Make up your own sentences for dictation activities using the focus phonemes.
- Ask more able writers to make up silly sentences for dictation, using the focus phonemes.
- Encourage story-telling through the use of puppets. This gives ideas for writing.

1. Say	s a t i p n c k ck e o r m d g u l h f b ai j oa ee z w oo (as in *wood*) oo (as in *cool*) ie v y (as in *yak*) ch sh th (as in *that*) th (as in *thank*) ng x qu ar er ou oi u-e or ay a-e ea y (as in *sunny*) igh i-e y (as in *fly*) ow (as in *snow*) o-e ew u-e ir ur au aw al oy ow (as in *cow*) air are
2. Blend	Focus phoneme groups for words: s a t i p n • c k ck e o r • m d g u l • h f b ai j • oa ee z w oo (short) • oo (long) ie v y (as in *yak*) ch • sh th (as in *that*) th (as in *thank*) ng x • qu ar er ou oi • ue or • ea y (as in *sunny*) • **igh i-e y** (as in *fly*) – **high sly cry fly sky dive time five hide light night time flight bright**
3. Chop	Focus phoneme groups for words: s a t i p n • c k ck e o r • m d g u l • h f b ai j • oa ee z w oo (short) • oo (long) ie v y (as in *yak*) ch • sh th (as in *that*) th (as in *thank*) ng x • qu ar er ou oi • ue or • ea y (as in *sunny*) • **igh i-e y** (as in *fly*) – **high sly cry fly sky dive time five hide light night time flight bright**
4. Fast words	I the • to was • he she • we said • you are • all they • my come • me go • like no • have be • by one • so some • little do her • did here there • saw when who • what where after • because want were • your two very • don't people many • more could should • would put brother • down love their • every likes

5. Read Reading sentences

Five men are stuck in the tree.
The flight to Spain took a long time.
A big cloud was high up in the sky.
I cry a lot if I am lost and alone.
The monster had five bright red teeth.

5. Write Writing sentences

I can fly my red kite high up.
Dive in the waves and have some fun.
The sly fox crept under the gate.
The North Star is very bright in the sky.
The time was late and the sky was dark.

Sessions 217–226

Tips

- Use drama across the curriculum to stimulate writing.
- Different groups of designers (children in role) talk about what they made in D & T.
- Make up your own sentences for dictation activities using the focus phonemes.
- Ask more able writers to make up silly sentences for dictation, using the focus phonemes.
- Ask children to make picture books about their favourite TV programme and to write captions.
- Some children may have moved beyond *Collins Big Cat Phonics Readers* blue level and be ready to choose appropriate books from *Collins Big Cat* to read independently.

1. Say	s a t i p n c k ck e o r m d g u l h f b ai j oa ee z w oo (as in *wood*) oo (as in *cool*) ie v y (as in *yak*) ch sh th (as in *that*) th (as in *thank*) ng x qu ar er ou oi u-e or ay a-e ea y (as in *sunny*) igh i-e y (as in *fly*) ow (as in *snow*) o-e ew u-e ir ur au aw al oy ow (as in *cow*) air are
2. Blend	Focus phoneme groups for words: s a t i p n • c k ck e o r • m d g u l • h f b ai j • oa ee z w oo (as in *wood*) • oo (as in *cool*) ie v y (as in *yak*) ch • sh th (as in *that*) th (as in *thank*) ng x • qu ar er ou oi • ue or • ea y (as in *sunny*) • igh i-e y (as in *fly*) • **ow** (as in *snow*) o-e – **hope row low show rose home woke crow those slow snow close smoke thrown**
3. Chop	Focus phoneme groups for words: s a t i p n • c k ck e o r • m d g u l • h f b ai j • oa ee z w oo (as in *wood*) • oo (as in *cool*) ie v y (as in *yak*) ch • sh th (as in *that*) th (as in *thank*) ng x • qu ar er ou oi • ue or • ea y (as in *sunny*) • igh i-e y (as in *fly*) • **ow** (as in *snow*) o-e – **hope row low show rose home woke crow those slow snow close smoke thrown**
4. Fast words	I the • to was • he she • we said • you are • all they • my come • me go • like no • have be • by one • so some • little do her • did here there • saw when who • what where after • because want were • your two very • don't people many • more could should • would put brother • down love their • every likes

5. Read Reading sentences

There are six black crows in the tree.
Who can show me the way home?
Thick smoke rose up in the sky.
Close the gate and come home!
The fox sank low in the grass when the farmer went past.

5. Write Writing sentences

I hope that the snow will stay all day.
I woke up very late on Sunday.
What is the name of that yellow rose?
Row the boat as fast as you can.
After dark, rubbish was thrown in my garden.

Sessions 227–236

Tips

- Ask the children to think of another sentence with different words, using the focus group of phonemes.
- Try a whole session at independent level.
- Use drama across the curriculum to stimulate writing; for example, write a letter from Jack to the giant apologising for stealing things; or an invitation from the witch in Hansel and Gretel to come to tea!
- Make up your own sentences for dictation activities using the focus phonemes.
- Ask more able writers to make up silly sentences for dictation, using the focus phonemes.
- Encourage children to use letter names when spelling fast words in their writing.
- Try Benchmark Assessment D on page 66 if they have made good progress.

1. Say	s a t i p n c k ck e o r m d g u l h f b ai j oa ee z w oo (as in *wood*) oo (as in *cool*) ie v y (as in *yak*) ch sh th (as in *that*) th (as in *thank*) ng x qu ar er ou oi u-e or ay a-e ea y (as in *sunny*) igh i-e y (as in *fly*) ow (as in *snow*) o-e ew u-e ir ur au aw al oy ow (as in *cow*) air are
2. Blend	Focus phoneme groups for words: s a t i p n • c k ck e o r • m d g u l • h f b ai j • oa ee z w oo (as in *wood*) • oo (as in *cool*) ie v y (as in *yak*) ch • sh th (as in *that*) th (as in *thank*) ng x • qu ar er ou oi • ue or • ea y (as in *sunny*) • igh i-e y (as in *fly*) • ow (as in *snow*) o-e • **ew u-e – few new use chew rude June tune blew grew threw**
3. Chop	Focus phoneme groups for words: s a t i p n • c k ck e o r • m d g u l • h f b ai j • oa ee z w oo (as in *wood*) • oo (as in *cool*) ie v y (as in *yak*) ch • sh th (as in *that*) th (as in *thank*) ng x • qu ar er ou oi • ue or • ea y (as in *sunny*) • igh i-e y (as in *fly*) • ow (as in *snow*) o-e • **ew u-e – few new use chew rude June tune blew grew threw**
4. Fast words	I the • to was • he she • we said • you are • all they • my come • me go • like no • have be • by one • so some • little do her • did here there • saw when who • what where after • because want were • your two very • don't people many • more could should • would put brother • down love their • every likes

5. Read Reading sentences	5. Write Writing sentences
Her new dress was made from pale pink silk. It is very rude to chew gum in class. We all want to see the new jazz band. My mum hums a tune when she makes supper. I threw it down because it was so hot.	There were few tickets left for the show. What do you use for cleaning black marks off hands? The strong wind blew the roof off her shed. The carrots grew well in the good soil. The twins will be six in June.

Benchmark Assessment D (see page 66)

DETAILED PROGRAMME OUTLINE

Sessions 237–246

Tips

- Use drama across the curriculum to stimulate writing; for example, write a postcard from Old Mother Hubbard to Little Red Riding Hood asking her to bring some food!
- Make up your own sentences for dictation activities using the focus phonemes.
- Ask more able writers to make up silly sentences for dictation using the focus phonemes.
- Begin to show children how to use dictionaries to find words.
- Some children may have moved beyond *Collins Big Cat Phonics Readers* blue level and be ready to choose appropriate books from *Collins Big Cat* to read independently.

1. Say	s a t i p n c k ck e o r m d g u l h f b ai j oa ee z w oo (as in *wood*) oo (as in *cool*) ie v y (as in *yak*) ch sh th (as in *that*) th (as in *thank*) ng x qu ar er ou oi u-e or ay a-e ea y (as in *sunny*) igh i-e y (as in *fly*) ow (as in *snow*) o-e ew u-e ir ur au aw al oy ow (as in *cow*) air are
2. Blend	Focus phoneme groups for words: s a t i p n • c k ck e o r • m d g u l • h f b ai j • oa ee z w oo (as in *wood*) • oo (as in *cool*) ie v y (as in *yak*) ch • sh th (as in *that*) th (as in *thank*) ng x • qu ar er ou oi • ue or • ea y (as in *sunny*) • igh i-e y (as in *fly*) • ow (as in *cow*) o-e • ew u-e • **ir ur – fir fur Sir bird burnt dirt girl turn shirt third stir skirt**
3. Chop	Focus phoneme groups for words: s a t i p n • c k ck e o r • m d g u l • h f b ai j • oa ee z w oo (as in *wood*) • oo (as in *cool*) ie v y (as in *yak*) ch • sh th (as in *that*) th (as in *thank*) ng x • qu ar er ou oi • ue or • ea y (as in *sunny*) • igh i-e y (as in *fly*) • ow (as in *cow*) o-e • ew u-e • **ir ur – fir fur Sir bird burnt dirt girl turn shirt third stir skirt**
4. Fast words	I the • to was • he she • we said • you are • all they • my come • me go • like no • have be • by one • so some • little do her • did here there • saw when who • what where after • because want were • your two very • don't people many • more could should • would put brother • down love their • every likes

5. Read Reading sentences	5. Write Writing sentences
It was safe for the bird to sit high up in the fir tree. Sir James came to meet the class. My cat came third in the cat show. People like to see shooting stars at night. I made a skirt from a bin bag.	Cats and dogs have very thick fur. I burnt the toast on Sunday. The little girl fell in the dirt and cried a lot. My dad likes a clean shirt every day. Stir the eggs in the pan, then add some pepper.

Sessions 247–256

Tips

- Try a whole session at both fully-supported and independent levels.
- Use drama across the curriculum to stimulate writing; for example, children draw and label a story map of Cinderella. Ask children in role as the Prince to present the map, and to say where they found Cinderella.
- Make up your own sentences for dictation activities using the focus phonemes.
- Ask more able writers to make up silly sentences for dictation using the focus phonemes.
- Some children may have moved beyond *Collins Big Cat Phonics Readers* blue level and be ready to choose appropriate books from *Collins Big Cat* to read independently.

1. Say	s a t i p n c k ck e o r m d g u l h f b ai j oa ee z w oo (as in *wood*) oo (as in *cool*) ie v y (as in *yak*) ch sh th (as in *that*) th (as in *thank*) ng x qu ar er ou oi u-e or ay a-e ea y (as in *sunny*) igh i-e y (as in *fly*) ow (as in *snow*) o-e ew u-e ir ur au aw al oy ow (as in *cow*) air are
2. Blend	Focus phoneme groups for words: s a t i p n • c k ck e o r • m d g u l • h f b ai j • oa ee z w oo (as in *wood*) • oo (as in *cool*) ie v y (as in *yak*) ch • sh th (as in *that*) th (as in *thank*) ng x • qu ar er ou oi • ue or • ea y (as in *sunny*) • igh i-e y (as in *fly*) • ow (as in *snow*) o-e • ew u-e • ir ur • **au aw al – jaw paw tall lawn Paul talk walk chalk shawl claw draw straw launch**
3. Chop	Focus phoneme groups for words: s a t i p n • c k ck e o r • m d g u l • h f b ai j • oa ee z w oo (as in *wood*) • oo (as in *cool*) ie v y (as in *yak*) ch • sh th (as in *that*) th (as in *thank*) ng x • qu ar er ou oi • ue or • ea y (as in *sunny*) • igh i-e y (as in *fly*) • ow (as in *snow*) o-e • ew u-e • ir ur • **au aw al – jaw paw tall lawn Paul talk walk chalk shawl claw draw straw launch**
4. Fast words	I the • to was • he she • we said • you are • all they • my come • me go • like no • have be • by one • so some • little do her • did here there • saw when who • what where after • because want were • your two very • don't people many • more could should • would put brother • down love their • every likes

5. Read Reading sentences

Sharks have big jaws with lots of sharp teeth.
Paul talks to his mates at playtime.
You can draw inside or outside.
I could ask for some chalk for drawing outside.
DO NOT WALK ON THE LAWN!

5. Write Writing sentences

All cats have soft paws and sharp claws.
It is good to walk home with Mum.
My gran gave me a shawl when I was little.
Straw is made from dried grass.
Paul is tall but I am small.

DETAILED PROGRAMME OUTLINE

Sessions 257–266

Tips

- Try a whole session at independent level.
- Play the *Treasure Island* and *Hide and Seek* activities on the CD-ROM.
- Use drama across the curriculum to stimulate writing; for example, children write in role as a character from a DVD, describing their plight and asking for help.
- Make up your own sentences for dictation activities using the focus phonemes.
- Ask more able writers to make up silly sentences for dictation, using the focus phonemes.
- Some children may have moved beyond *Collins Big Cat Phonics Readers* blue level and be ready to choose appropriate books from *Collins Big Cat* to read independently.
- See if more children are ready to move into your guided reading programme.

1. Say	s a t i p n c k ck e o r m d g u l h f b ai j oa ee z w oo (as in *wood*) oo (as in *cool*) ie v y (as in *yak*) ch sh th (as in *that*) th (as in *thank*) ng x qu ar er ou oi u-e or ay a-e ea y (as in *sunny*) igh i-e y (as in *fly*) ow (as in *snow*) o-e ew u-e ir ur au aw al oy ow (as in *cow*) air are
2. Blend	Focus phoneme groups for words: s a t i p n • c k ck e o r • m d g u l • h f b ai j • oa ee z w oo (as in *wood*) • oo (as in *cool*) ie v y (as in *yak*) ch • sh th (as in *that*) th (as in *thank*) ng x • qu ar er ou oi • ue or • ea y (as in *sunny*) • igh i-e y (as in *fly*) • ow (as in *snow*) o-e • ew u-e • ir ur • au aw al • **oy ow** (as in *cow*) – **boy toy Roy cow how now row down gown town brown crown clown growl**
3. Chop	Focus phoneme groups for words: s a t i p n • c k ck e o r • m d g u l • h f b ai j • oa ee z w oo (as in *wood*) • oo (as in *cool*) ie v y (as in *yak*) ch • sh th (as in *that*) th (as in *thank*) ng x • qu ar er ou oi • ue or • ea y (as in *sunny*) • igh i-e y (as in *fly*) • ow (as in *snow*) o-e • ew u-e • ir ur • au aw al • **oy ow** (as in *cow*) – **boy toy Roy cow how now row down gown town brown crown clown growl**
4. Fast words	I the • to was • he she • we said • you are • all they • my come • me go • like no • have be • by one • so some • little do her • did here there • saw when who • what where after • because want were • your two very • don't people many • more could should • would put brother • down love their • every likes

5. Read Reading sentences

Roy is my pet tawny owl.
The boy saw lots of people in town.
People have been up and down hills on the moon.
I had a big row with the girl who hit me.
The growling dog had big teeth.

5. Write Writing sentences

All owls have very sharp claws.
Cows like eating fresh green grass.
My mum wants me to pick up my toys.
The clown had a red nose and a big smile.
The king had a little crown on.

Sessions 267–276

Tips

- Try a whole session at independent level.
- Some children may have moved beyond *Collins Big Cat Phonics Readers* blue level and be ready to choose appropriate books from *Collins Big Cat* to read independently.
- Let children in 'reading time' choose a book to read aloud to a group. Video some of this for children to watch and discuss.
- Ask children to make up decodable stories using only the phonemes and fast words you give them!
- Play the *Treasure Island* and *Hide and Seek* activities on the CD-ROM.
- Make up your own sentences for dictation activities using the focus phonemes.

1. Say	s a t i p n c k ck e o r m d g u l h f b ai j oa ee z w oo (as in *wood*) oo (as in *cool*) ie v y (as in *yak*) ch sh th (as in *that*) th (as in *thank*) ng x qu ar er ou oi u-e or ay a-e ea y (as in *sunny*) igh i-e y (as in *fly*) ow (as in *snow*) o-e ew u-e ir ur au aw al oy ow (as in *cow*) air are
2. Blend	Focus phoneme groups for words: s a t i p n • c k ck e o r • m d g u l • h f b ai j • oa ee z w oo (as in *wood*) • oo (as in *cool*) ie v y (as in *yak*) ch • sh th (as in *that*) th (as in *thank*) ng x • qu ar er ou oi • ue or • ea y (as in *sunny*) • igh i-e y (as in *fly*) • ow (as in *snow*) o-e • ew u-e • ir ur • au aw al • oy ow (as in *cow*) • **air are – dare hare mare hair pair chair stair glare**
3. Chop	Focus phoneme groups for words: s a t i p n • c k ck e o r • m d g u l • h f b ai j • oa ee z w oo (as in *wood*) • oo (as in *cool*) ie v y (as in *yak*) ch • sh th (as in *that*) th (as in *thank*) ng x • qu ar er ou oi • ue or • ea y (as in *sunny*) • igh i-e y (as in *fly*) • ow (as in *snow*) o-e • ew u-e • ir ur • au aw al • oy ow (as in *cow*) • **air are – dare hare mare hair pair chair stair glare**
4. Fast words	I the • to was • he she • we said • you are • all they • my come • me go • like no • have be • by one • so some • little do her • did here there • saw when who • what where after • because want were • your two very • don't people many • more could should • would put brother • down love their • every likes

5. Read Reading sentences

How dare you eat my last sweet!
The mad hare sat in his chair for his tea.
The hares were boxing in the grass!
Do not fall down the steep stairs.
The chair was made from very hard wood.

5. Write Writing sentences

A hare can run much faster than a fox.
The chair was bigger than they were.
The big mare can jump high.
She gave me a glare when she saw my green hair.
She broke the chair and then went to bed.

DETAILED PROGRAMME OUTLINE

> The remaining 23 sessions offer more practice using a range of phonemes, words and sentences.

Sessions 277–286

Tips

- Ask the children to think of another sentence with different words, using the focus group of phonemes.
- Use drama across the curriculum to stimulate writing; for example, children in role as famous historical characters are interviewed by the class. Children write notes, saying what they liked about the activity they saw.
- Make up your own sentences for dictation activities using the focus phonemes.
- Ask more able writers to make up silly sentences for dictation, using the focus phonemes.
- Some children may have moved beyond *Collins Big Cat Phonics Readers* blue level and be ready to choose appropriate books from *Collins Big Cat* to read independently.
- Try a whole session at independent level.

1. Say	s a t i p n c k ck e o r m d g u l h f b ai j oa ee z w oo (as in *wood*) oo (as in *cool*) ie v y (as in *yak*) ch sh th (as in *that*) th (as in *thank*) ng x qu ar er ou oi u-e or ay a-e ea y (as in *sunny*) igh i-e y (as in *fly*) ow (as in *snow*) o-e ew u-e ir ur au aw al oy ow (as in *cow*) air are
2. Blend *All phonemes are now used for blending words*	Focus phoneme groups for words: s a t i p n • c k ck e o r • m d g u l • h f b ai j • oa ee z w oo (as in *wood*) • oo (as in *cool*) ie v y (as in *yak*) ch • sh th (as in *that*) th (as in *thank*) ng x • qu ar er ou oi • ue or • ea y (as in *sunny*) • igh i-e y (as in *fly*) • ow (as in *snow*) o-e • ew u-e • ir ur • au aw al • oy ow (as in *cow*) • air are **stole night cakes smelly buggy loud fright funny bang slide names clouds cubes picnic lawn**
3. Chop *All phonemes are now used for blending words*	Focus phoneme groups for words: s a t i p n • c k ck e o r • m d g u l • h f b ai j • oa ee z w oo (as in *wood*) • oo (as in *cool*) ie v y (as in *yak*) ch • sh th (as in *that*) th (as in *thank*) ng x • qu ar er ou oi • ue or • ea y (as in *sunny*) • igh i-e y (as in *fly*) • ow (as in *snow*) o-e • ew u-e • ir ur • au aw al • oy ow (as in *cow*) • air are **stole night cakes smelly buggy loud fright funny bang slide names clouds cubes picnic lawn**
4. Fast words	I the • to was • he she • we said • you are • all they • my come • me go • like no • have be • by one • so some • little do her • did here there • saw when who • what where after • because want were • your two very • don't people many • more could should • would put brother • down love their • every likes

5. Read Reading sentences

He stole the cakes from my plate.
Mum lost the buggy and Jane had to walk home.
The loud bang gave me a big fright.
Who has a funny joke to tell?
Could you put five cubes in the box for me?

5. Write Writing sentences

I had a good dream last night – did you?
I found my smelly socks under the bed.
When can I go down the slide and into the deep pool?
What are the names of those clowns?
I never came first in the fun runs.

Sessions 287–299

Tips

- Try a whole session at independent level.
- Play the *Bubbles* and *Hide and Seek* activities on the CD-ROM.
- Use drama across the curriculum to stimulate writing; for example, re-telling a story in role to a friend, then writing it.
- Make up your own sentences for dictation activities using the focus phonemes.
- Ask more able writers to make up silly sentences for dictation, using the focus phonemes.
- Some children may have moved beyond *Collins Big Cat Phonics Readers* blue level and be ready to choose appropriate books from *Collins Big Cat* to read independently.

1. Say	s a t i p n c k ck e o r m d g u l h f b ai j oa ee z w oo (as in *wood*) oo (as in *cool*) ie v y (as in *yak*) ch sh th (as in *that*) th (as in *thank*) ng x qu ar er ou oi u-e or ay a-e ea y (as in *sunny*) igh i-e y (as in *fly*) ow (as in *snow*) o-e ew u-e ir ur au aw al oy ow (as in *cow*) air are
2. Blend	Focus phoneme groups for words: s a t i p n • ck ck e o r • m d g u l • h f b ai j • oa ee z w oo (as in *wood*) • oo (as in *cool*) ie v y (as in *yak*) ch • sh th (as in *that*) th (as in *thank*) ng x • qu ar er ou oi • ue or • ea y (as in *sunny*) • igh i-e y (as in *fly*) • ow (as in *snow*) o-e • ew u-e • ir ur • au aw al • oy ow (as in *cow*) • air are **walks sunny unhappy gown silk loudly glare green beans brown silly party glass shoot train**
3. Chop	Focus phoneme groups for words: s a t i p n • ck ck e o r • m d g u l • h f b ai j • oa ee z w oo (as in *wood*) • oo (as in *cool*) ie v y (as in *yak*) ch • sh th (as in *that*) th (as in *thank*) ng x • qu ar er ou oi • ue or • ea y (as in *sunny*) • igh i-e y (as in *fly*) • ow (as in *snow*) o-e • ew u-e • ir ur • au aw al • oy ow (as in *cow*) • air are **walks sunny unhappy gown silk loudly glare green beans brown silly party glass shoot train**
4. Fast words	I the • to was • he she • we said • you are • all they • my come • me go • like no • have be • by one • so some • little do her • did here there • saw when who • what where after • because want were • your two very • don't people many • more could should • would put brother • down love their • every likes

5. Read Reading sentences	5. Write Writing sentences
We all had a picnic on the lawn. The king was rich but very unhappy. The little boy can howl very loudly. Green beans are good for you. I had a silly hat on for the party. The red train was very slow. I can shoot the ball into the net.	When it is sunny we all go for walks. The girl had a ball gown made from silk. Don't glare at me like that! The brown ants made a big nest. The best gift I had from my gran was a kiss! The tree was made from glass.

Benchmark Assessment E (see page 67)

Session 300

This session ends the programme with farewells from Snappy and Big Cat.

Collins Big Cat and synthetic phonics

Synthetic phonics is used throughout *Collins Big Cat Phonics*. This means that children are taught the most common letter-sound combinations first. These small units of sound are called **phonemes**. They then use these to blend and segment words. Children learn in small steps, each step building on the one before.

Common terms

Blending is the synthesizing, or combining, of phonemes in the order they occur along a word to read it:

c a t = cat

Segmenting is the breaking up of a word into its phonemes in the order they occur along a word to spell it:

cat = c a t

Common terms

A **phoneme** is another word for a sound. The sound may have more than one grapheme or letter. You can choose which term – phoneme or sound – to use with the children. *Collins Big Cat Phonics* refers to sounds.

A **grapheme** is another term for a letter or collection of letters.

A **sound button** is a dot which appears under each individual phoneme. This shows the children which phoneme to say aloud as they blend along the word in reading, or segment it for spelling.

sat

Finger pointing. In blending, model for the children how to use a 'pointing finger'. Say and point at each phoneme, then finish by sweeping your finger along, under the word.

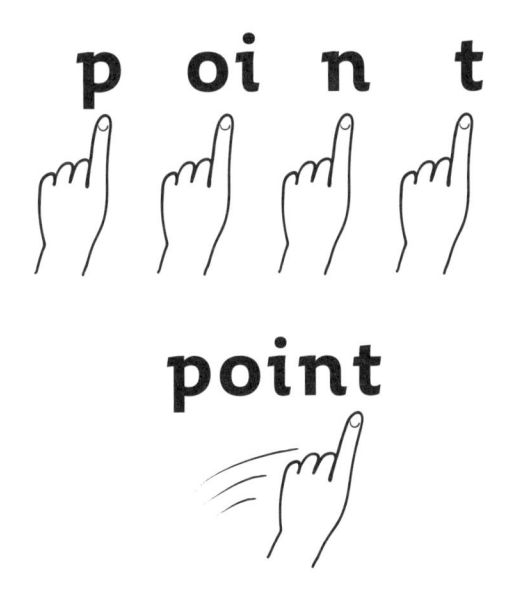

p oi n t

point

Finger counting: In segmenting, model how to say the words, then, starting with your thumb, count each phoneme out on your fingers as you move along the word.

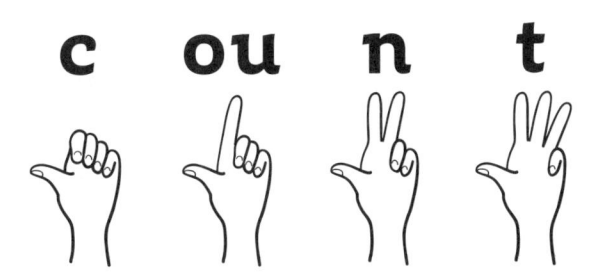

c ou n t

Phonemes or sounds in *Collins Big Cat Phonics*

Children learn to say, read and write the following phonemes in *Collins Big Cat Phonics*. These cover all the major letter-sound combinations in the English language.

These phonemes are introduced one at a time between Sessions 1 and 42, and then practised.

s a t i p n

c k ck e o r

m d g u l

h f b ai j

oa ee z w oo (as in *wood*)

oo (as in *cool*) **ie v y** (as in *yak*) **ch**

sh th (as in *that*) **th** (as in *thank*) **ng x**

qu ar er ou oi

u-e or

These phonemes are introduced one at a time between Sessions 150 and 169, and then practised along with the earlier phonemes.

ay a-e

ea y (as in *sunny*)

igh i-e y (as in *fly*)

ow (as in *snow*) **o-e**

ew ue

ir ur

au aw al

oy ow (as in *cow*)

air are

How to say the sounds

It's important to pronounce the sounds correctly. Be careful not to end a sound with an unnecessary 'uh'. Say 'c' not 'cuh', 'sss' not 'suh', 'lll' not 'luh' and 'mmm' not 'muh'. Avoiding the 'uh' sound makes it easier for children to hear the pure sound, which makes it easier for them to blend and segment. Try to end the sound crisply and cleanly.

✗ cuh a tuh

✓ c a t

Some sounds like 'b', 'd' and 'g' do have an 'uh' sound when they are pronounced.

The sounds are all correctly modelled in *Collins Big Cat Phonics* by Big Cat and Snappy.

Confusables

Some phonemes share the same grapheme or letters, but sound different.

oo   Short: w**oo**d
       Long: c**oo**l

th   Voiced: **th**at
       Unvoiced: **th**ank.

y   As in **y**ak, sunn**y**, or fl**y**.

ow   Short: sn**ow**
       Long: c**ow**.

Go to page 19 for ideas on how to use this in the classroom.

Double consonant letters (such as ss, ll, ff): These are pronounced as one sound (s, l, f).

*The phoneme **y** has three different sounds, as in **y**ak, fl**y** and sunn**y**, and as illustrated on the CD-Rom.*

Collins Big Cat Phonics and assessment

This handbook offers you very practical guidance on assessing children during the daily 10-minute session, as well as at other times. Children will progress at different rates through this programme. Continuous assessment shows you what progress each child is making and helps you to identify their strengths and weaknesses.

Assessment through observation

Quick assessment of whole class progress

You can assess children's progress at any stage of *Collins Big Cat Phonics* by using the independent level for Say, Blend, Chop, and Fast words. This is when children see the phonemes or words and say, blend or segment them without any support from the characters.

Quick assessment of small group progress

You can assess more easily if you group the children according to ability. This allows you to target a few words at certain groups while the rest remain silent. You may do this for one section, for example blending, or for more than one, such as blending and reading the sentence at the end of the session. An average class is likely to consist of one more able group, one struggling group and three average groups.

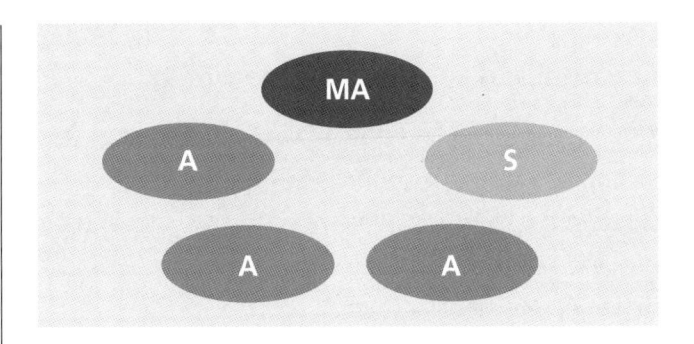

Move around the groups each day, targeting the **more able (MA)**, **average (A)** and **struggling (S)** groups in turn. Keep a record of children's progress, like the one below.

A tick shows that a group got more than 75% of answers correct. A cross indicates that less than 25% of answers were correct.

1 = Say 2 = Blend 3 = Chop 4 = Fast words 5R = Read 5W = Write							
Date	Group(s)	Progress						
16 Jan.	MA	1 ✓	2 ✓	3 ✓	4 ✓	5R ✓	5W ✓
17 Jan.	A	1 ✓	2 ✓	3 ✓	4 ✗	5R	5W ✗
18 Jan.	S	1 ✓	2 ✓	3 ✗	4 ✗	5R ✗	5W

Individual assessment

Photocopiable sheets are provided on pages 63–67 and 69–76 for you or a teaching assistant to use while the session is running. You can observe one child for each part of the session.

You may observe children who you think are making good progress and may soon be ready for the first set of *Collins Big Cat Phonics Readers*. You can also observe children who appear to be making little progress. Those children who are making little or very slow progress should be assessed individually by you, using the appropriate Benchmark Assessment on pages 63–67.

Personalised teaching and learning

Share with each child how well they are doing, for example how many sounds they know, how they can blend cvc words, remember fast words, and so on, and tell them that Big Cat and Snappy would be very pleased with them!

Five benchmarks for assessment

Collins Big Cat Phonics provides you with five photocopiable Benchmark Assessments on pages 63–67. These match different stages of the programme and can be used with individual children. Use these for more detailed feedback on what a child can or can't yet do. The Benchmark Assessments also suggest ideas for next steps.

Use Benchmark Assessment A to identify children who are struggling early on, and Benchmark Assessments B–E to identify children who are underattaining in the later stages of the programme. Ask the following questions:

- How many phonemes does the child know?
- How many words can the child blend?
- How many words can the child segment?
- How many fast words does the child know?

If the answer to a question is less than 25% over two assessments follow the relevant Next steps advice on pages 61–62.

Extra sessions for struggling children

It can benefit those children who are struggling to practise the session in a small group with you or the teaching assistant. You can add variety to this extra session by building in activities included on the CD-ROM.

Children who are not yet ready for *Collins Big Cat Phonics* can use lilac and pink level *Collins Big Cat* reading books. These books will stimulate their talk and interest. Ideas and support for speaking, listening and comprehension are at the back of each book.

Splitting the class

If some children are racing ahead, consider splitting the class and using different stages of *Collins Big Cat Phonics* with each group.

> **If a child is inattentive and lacks concentration early on, it may be better to start them on the programme later, when they are able to sit still and take an active part.**
>
> **If a child appears to know the sounds but can't blend, check their hearing – intermittent deafness due to ear infections may mean the child can't hear right across the words. This may also cause the inattentiveness described above. Children who peer closely at books to scan pictures and work on words may have an eyesight problem. Alert their carer if this is the case.**

Assessing reading skills

The Reading assessment support section on page 68 offers you guidance on:

- what to do with children who aren't ready for *Collins Big Cat Phonics Readers*
- what to listen for and observe while children are reading *Collins Big Cat Phonics Readers*.

Successful readers

All *Collins Big Cat Phonics Readers* offer practical advice on how to use the books with groups of children at the back of the book. Constructive guidance is given for developing children's vocabulary and comprehension. There are also extension activities which can be used independently by the children.

Readers without home support

These children will of course have your support as they read to you, individually or in small groups. If they are doing well, but have little support at home, give them plenty of opportunities to explore books and develop their tastes as readers through increased access to the school library and a range of reading experiences, including ICT.

Struggling readers need to read to someone every day to apply the skills learnt from the programme. Think of creative ways to do this, including using peer support.

Paired reading

Paired reading is a useful strategy if you can't get adult support to listen to struggling children read. Children in your class who are reading two levels higher or more can listen to and support a struggling reader. As they help the child attack words the child is stuck on, they are consolidating their own reading skills. This is a partnership with mutual benefits.

If the child has poor language skills and book knowledge, use the early *Collins Big Cat* pink and red level books to develop language skills and an appetite for reading. Children who are learning English as an additional language may also benefit from using these books as a supplement to build up their bank of language structures and vocabulary.

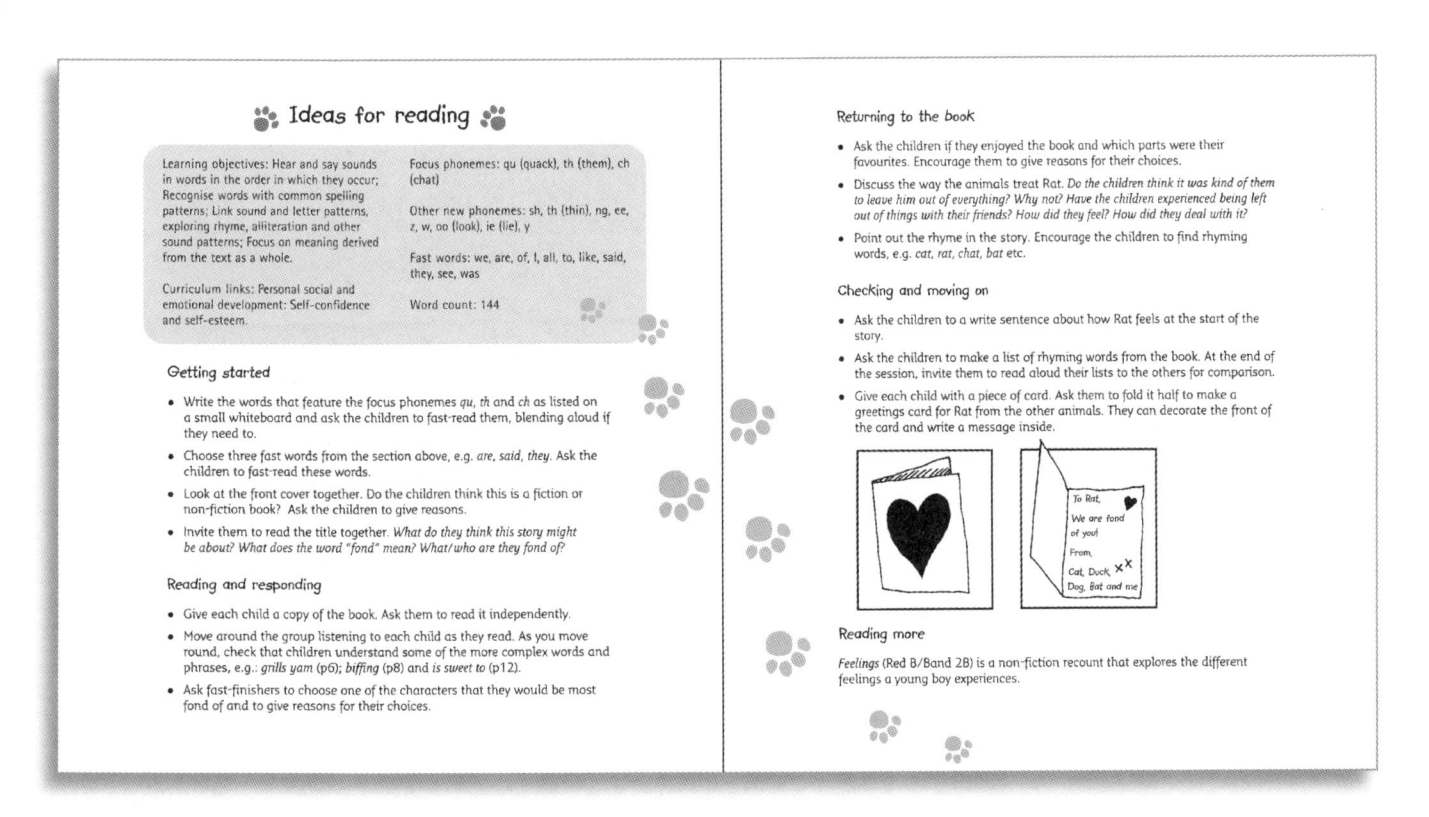

Ideas for reading

Learning objectives: Hear and say sounds in words in the order in which they occur; Recognise words with common spelling patterns; Link sound and letter patterns, exploring rhyme, alliteration and other sound patterns; Focus on meaning derived from the text as a whole.

Curriculum links: Personal social and emotional development: Self-confidence and self-esteem.

Focus phonemes: qu (quack), th (them), ch (chat)

Other new phonemes: sh, th (thin), ng, ee, z, w, oo (look), ie (lie), y

Fast words: we, are, of, I, all, to, like, said, they, see, was

Word count: 144

Getting started

- Write the words that feature the focus phonemes *qu*, *th* and *ch* as listed on a small whiteboard and ask the children to fast-read them, blending aloud if they need to.
- Choose three fast words from the section above, e.g. *are, said, they*. Ask the children to fast-read these words.
- Look at the front cover together. Do the children think this is a fiction or non-fiction book? Ask the children to give reasons.
- Invite them to read the title together. What do they think this story might be about? What does the word "fond" mean? What/who are they fond of?

Reading and responding

- Give each child a copy of the book. Ask them to read it independently.
- Move around the group listening to each child as they read. As you move round, check that children understand some of the more complex words and phrases, e.g. *grills yam* (p6); *biffing* (p8) and *is sweet to* (p12).
- Ask fast-finishers to choose one of the characters that they would be most fond of and to give reasons for their choices.

Returning to the book

- Ask the children if they enjoyed the book and which parts were their favourites. Encourage them to give reasons for their choices.
- Discuss the way the animals treat Rat. Do the children think it was kind of them to leave him out of everything? Why not? Have the children experienced being left out of things with their friends? How did they feel? How did they deal with it?
- Point out the rhyme in the story. Encourage the children to find rhyming words, e.g. *cat, rat, chat, bat* etc.

Checking and moving on

- Ask the children to a write sentence about how Rat feels at the start of the story.
- Ask the children to make a list of rhyming words from the book. At the end of the session, invite them to read aloud their lists to the others for comparison.
- Give each child with a piece of card. Ask them to fold it half to make a greetings card for Rat from the other animals. They can decorate the front of the card and write a message inside.

Reading more

Feelings (Red B/Band 2B) is a non-fiction recount that explores the different feelings a young boy experiences.

Assessing writing skills

The Writing Assessment Support sheets (pages 69–71) provide guidance on recognising key developmental stages and what to do next. They give examples of children's early attempts at writing, from a wavy line to represent words, to good phonetic spelling and improved recall of irregular words. By collecting examples of independent writing from children on a regular basis, you will see the impact of the daily 10-minute session.

Children starting school at the age of four will vary enormously in their ability to write and spell. A typical class is likely to have children represented throughout all three stages shown on page 69. The three stages are:

- Emerging
- Developing
- Taking off

Some children may still be at the pre-emergent stage where they have no idea about writing and are making random marks on paper. Others (likely to be very few) may be able to construct a whole text, mostly correctly spelled, and be further on than the *Taking off* stage.

Using the assessment sheets

When you assess a child's writing and spelling, compare the examples on pages 69–71 with their independent writing. Tick the stage they are at. They may be between two stages. Whichever stage(s) they are at, follow the advice to help them move into the next stage.

Some children will move on quickly and others slowly. Slower pupils will benefit from more time with an adult, for example making little books together about things which interest them.

Remember

- Some children may stick at one stage for a long time, then suddenly move on.
- Some children will fly through these stages and 'take off' with ease.
- Some children will jump stages.
- Some children will need lots of support, and others very little.
- In all cases, daily practice at segmenting words is vital, as is the demonstration writing section (Write) at the end of the 10-minute session.

Tips

- Children need a real purpose for writing.
- Create an attractive writing area with a variety of writing tools and materials.
- Provide a consistent approach to teaching handwriting.

Through regular observation of independent writing you will see the impact of the daily 10-minute phonics session.

Next steps

If children are scoring 25% or less after two benchmark assessments, give them small group or individual practice of the sounds and words they've learned using the following suggestions. Also check the child's hearing and eyesight with their carer.

Phonemes

The child has limited recognition when seeing these on screen and trying to blend along a word is hampered by their limited knowledge of phonemes.

Multi-sensory strategies

- Model one-to-one, with you saying and mouthing the sounds.
- Use a mirror for them to see the sound being made.
- Practise drawing letter shapes using sky-writing, in sand, paint, finger painting, 'feely' letters or tracing.
- It can help to join up the letters for digraphs, to show that these are made up of two letters which have one sound, for example

ai oa ee oo

- Sort sounds into sets, by posting words written on cards which have the same first, middle or last sound into appropriately labelled boxes, for example: b = box, bat; s = sat, sit; ee = sheep, feel; o = cot, Tom; t = fat, lit; p = tap, lip.
- Make up sets of these 'posting words' with 12 words in a set.
- Use *Collins Big Cat Phonics* activities for letter sounds, names and shapes practice.

Blending

The child has limited success when blending; they can recognise and say individual phonemes, but can't blend along a whole word and will give up too soon.

Oral blending along the names of objects

- Fill a bag with six real objects, such as a tin, a toy cat, and so on. As you take each one out of the bag in turn, say, in a surprised manner, 'Oh, it's a t-i-n tin!'. Encourage the children to join in with you. Then ask them to join in again as you put each one back in the bag.

Using a robot-style voice

- Play the same game as above using a hand puppet and a robot-style voice. Tell the children the puppet knows the sounds but can't blend and ask for their help. The puppet (you) says 'c-a-t' in the robot-style voice, and the children copy and blend, saying 'c-a-t cat'.

Stretching words

- Say the sounds in cvc words as if they are stretched out, for example, 'sssssss-aaaaa-ttttt – sat'.

Rainbow blending

- Arrange plastic or magnetic letters of the alphabet in a semi-circle, like a rainbow. Put down a consonant, then a vowel, then a consonant to make a word. Ask them to choose a consonant, you choose a vowel, they choose a consonant. It doesn't matter if it doesn't make a real word. Ask them to sound out and blend the 'word'. Praise them for making and blending along a 'silly word'. You can use *Collins Big Cat Phonics* activity *Rainbow Letters* for this too.

Practising consonant clusters at the beginning of words

- Ask the children to say the second letter louder, for example: c-**l**-a-p; s-**p**-i-n; t-**r**-a-i-n.

Speedy blending

- Make some cards with consonant clusters for speedy visual recognition practice, for example: *cl*, *sp*, *nk*. Show the children each one in turn, to call out as a blend.
- Play the *Jack and the Beanstalk* and *Hide and Seek* activities on the CD-ROM.

Segmenting

The child has limited success when segmenting; they can say some or all of the phonemes, but still have difficulty in writing these phonemes down, working across the word. They leave some out, or write the first sound only.

Scribe for the child

- Scribe for the child, describing what you are doing as you segment along words.

Say words aloud and use multi-sensory strategies

- Say a word, then write it with the child, holding their hand as you segment; you can use sky-writing, sand, paint, finger painting, 'feely' letters or tracing.

Phoneme checklists for spelling

- Make a small table-top card containing a phoneme checklist for individual children to refer to as they write both with you, and then later on their own.

Dictation

- Dictate words and watch the child write these on the whiteboard. Check their pen(cil) hold and individual letter formation. Hold their hand and practise with them.
- Dictate sentences. Help the child a little by segmenting words for them and telling them where the punctuation goes. Build their confidence – don't treat dictation like a test!

Practising consonant clusters

- Make sure the child segments each sound in a cluster, for example, not cl-a-p but c-l-a-p.

Rainbow segmenting

- Arrange plastic or magnetic letters of the alphabet in a semi-circle, like a rainbow. Call out a word for the children who pull down the letters as they segment. You can use *Collins Big Cat Phonics* activity *Rainbow Letters* for this too.
- Play the *Bubbles* activity on the CD-ROM.

Fast words

The child has limited success at recognising fast words on screen and in sentences.

Matching pairs

- Write up to 12 fast words from the appropriate level onto cards, with each word on two cards. Place them face down on the table, then look for matching pairs by turning the cards over, two at a time.

Sky-writing fast words

- Practise sky-writing whole words; you can also use sand, paint, finger painting, 'feely' letters or tracing.

Saying letter names

- Spell words aloud by saying (not sounding) individual letters, at speed, as they see the word (this supports spelling, not reading).

Dictation on small whiteboards

- Call out individual words for children to write in a joined hand, as fast as possible.

Benchmark Assessment A

Go to www.collinsbigcat.com to download free phoneme and word lists to use.

Pupil name _____   Date _____

Phonemes	Blending	Segmenting	Fast words
Circle the correct response.	Say aloud the phonemes in each word and ask the child to verbally blend them into a word. ✓ / ✗ Write what they say for incorrect blending.	Say each word, ask the child to segment it and write down the word on a small whiteboard. ✓ / ✗ Write what they say for incorrect segmenting. Copy what they write for incorrect segmenting.	Circle the correct response.
s a t i p n c k ck e o r m d g u l h f b ai j	s-a-t t-i-n p-a-n t-a-p a-n-t s-i-t p-i-n p-a-t n-i-p s-n-a-p	sat tin pan tap ant sit pin pat nip snap	I the to was

Collins Big Cat Phonics Handbook © HarperCollins*Publishers* 2006. This page may be photocopied for use in the classroom.

Benchmark Assessment B

Go to www.collinsbigcat.com to download free phoneme and word lists to use.

Pupil name _____   Date _____

Phonemes		Blending	Segmenting	Fast words
Circle the correct response.		Say aloud the phonemes in each word and ask the child to verbally blend them into a word. ✓ / ✗ Write what they say for incorrect blending.	Say each word, ask the child to segment it and write down the word on a small whiteboard. ✓ / ✗ Write what they say for incorrect segmenting. Copy what they write for incorrect segmenting.	Circle the correct response.
s	oa	j-e-t	jet	I
a	ee			the
t	z			to
i	w			was
p	oo (wood)	t-o-p	top	he
n	oo (cool)			she
c	ie			we
k	v	n-e-s-t	nest	said
ck	y (yak)			you
e	ch			are
o	sh	m-e-ss	mess	all
r	th (that)			they
m	th (thank)	d-u-ck	duck	my
d	ng			come
g	x			me
u	qu	p-u-ff	puff	go
l	ar			like
h	er	s-l-u-g	slug	no
f	ou	g-r-a-b	grab	have
b	oi	l-a-n-d	land	be
ai	ue			by
j	or	S-p-ai-n	Spain	one
				so
				some

Benchmark Assessment C

Go to www.collinsbigcat.com to download free phoneme and word lists to use.

Pupil name _____   Date _____

Phonemes	Blending	Segmenting	Fast words
Circle the correct response.	Say aloud the phonemes in each word and ask the child to verbally blend them into a word. ✓ / ✗ Write what they say for incorrect blending.	Say each word, ask the child to segment it and write down the word on a small whiteboard. ✓ / ✗ Write what they say for incorrect segmenting. Copy what they write for incorrect segmenting.	Circle the correct response.
s oa ay			I little
a ee a-e			the do
t z ea			to her
i w y (sunny)	Z-a-p	Zap	was did
p oo (wood) igh			he here
n oo (cool) i-e	v-a-n	van	she there
c ie y (fly)			we saw
k v ow (snow)	f-ee-l	feel	said when
ck y (yak) o-e			you who
e ch ew			are what
o sh u-e	w-oo-d	wood	all where
r th (that) ir			they after
m th (thank) ur	t-ee-th	teeth	my because
d ng au			come want
g x aw	ch-i-m-p	chimp	me were
u qu al			go your
l ar oy	b-r-u-sh	brush	like two
h er ow (cow)			no very
f ou air	f-ou-n-d	found	have don't
b oi are			be people
ai ue	s-m-ar-t	smart	by many
j or			one more
			so could
	sh-or-t-er	shorter	some should

Collins Big Cat Phonics Handbook   © HarperCollins*Publishers* 2006. This page may be photocopied for use in the classroom.

Benchmark Assessment D

Go to www.collinsbigcat.com to download free phoneme and word lists to use.

Pupil name _____   Date _____

Phonemes			Blending	Segmenting	Fast words	
Circle the correct response.			Say aloud the phonemes in each word and ask the child to verbally blend them into a word. ✓ / ✗ Write what they say for incorrect blending.	Say each word, ask the child to segment it and write down the word on a small whiteboard. ✓ / ✗ Write what they say for incorrect segmenting. Copy what they write for incorrect segmenting.	Circle the correct response.	
s	oa	ay			I	here
a	ee	a-e			the	there
t	z	ea			to	saw
i	w	y (sunny)	n-ew	new	was	when
p	oo (wood)	igh			he	who
n	oo (cool)	i-e	c-r-y	cry	she	what
c	ie	y (fly)			we	where
k	v	ow (snow)	d-are	dare	said	after
ck	y (yak)	o-e			you	because
e	ch	ew	l-igh-t	light	are	want
o	sh	u-e	s-n-ea-k	sneak	all	were
r	th (that)	ir			they	your
m	th (thank)	ur	g-l-are	glare	my	two
d	ng	au	c-a-ke	cake	come	very
g	x	aw			me	don't
u	qu	al	d-i-ve	dive	go	people
l	ar	oy	w-o-ke	woke	like	many
h	er	ow (cow)			no	more
f	ou	air	t-u-ne	tune	have	could
b	oi	are	b-ur-n-t	burnt	be	should
ai	ue				by	would
j	or		th-r-ow-n	thrown	one	put
					so	brother
					some	down
					little	love
					do	their
					her	every
					did	likes

Benchmark Assessment E

Go to www.collinsbigcat.com to download free phoneme and word lists to use.

Collins Big Cat Phonics

Pupil name _____   Date _____

Phonemes	Blending	Segmenting	Fast words
Circle the correct response.	Say aloud the phonemes in each word and ask the child to verbally blend them into a word. ✓ / ✗ Write what they say for incorrect blending.	Say each word, ask the child to segment it and write down the word on a small whiteboard. ✓ / ✗ Write what they say for incorrect segmenting. Copy what they write for incorrect segmenting.	Circle the correct response.

Phonemes			Blending	Segmenting	Fast words	
s	oa	ay			I	here
a	ee	a-e			the	there
t	z	ea			to	saw
i	w	y (sunny)	n-ew	new	was	when
p	oo (wood)	igh			he	who
n	oo (cool)	i-e	c-r-y	cry	she	what
c	ie	y (fly)			we	where
k	v	ow (snow)	d-are	dare	said	after
ck	y (yak)	o-e			you	because
e	ch	ew	l-igh-t	light	are	want
o	sh	u-e			all	were
r	th (that)	ir	s-n-ea-k	sneak	they	your
m	th (thank)	ur			my	two
d	ng	au	g-l-are	glare	come	very
g	x	aw			me	don't
u	qu	al	c-a-ke	cake	go	people
l	ar	oy			like	many
h	er	ow (cow)	d-i-ve	dive	no	more
f	ou	air			have	could
b	oi	are	w-o-ke	woke	be	should
ai	ue				by	would
j	or		t-u-ne	tune	one	put
					so	brother
			b-ur-n-t	burnt	some	down
					little	love
			th-r-ow-n	thrown	do	their
					her	every
					did	likes

Collins Big Cat Phonics Handbook © HarperCollinsPublishers 2006. This page may be photocopied for use in the classroom.

Reading assessment support

Use Benchmark Assessment A to see if a child is ready for *Collins Big Cat Phonics Readers* Red A. Red B Readers link to Benchmark Assessment B, Yellow Readers to Benchmark Assessment C and Blue Readers to Benchmark Assessment D.

When they encounter unknown words the child:	Support tips for a child who is struggling	Next steps for a child who is fluent, accurate and comprehends well
Recognises and says the first sound and moves along the word, sounding out words and blending and saying the whole word correctly.	• Do not prompt them when they are trying to work on a word – allow some time to listen to what they are doing. • If they don't apply good blending skills, prompt them to break the word into phonemes and blend together from left to right across the whole word (NB this doesn't apply to irregular words). • If they blended incorrectly, give the child time to self-correct, when they may be pulling in other reading strategies, e.g. word order or meaning linked to context. • If the child doesn't self-correct, expect them to do a re-run of the sentence when meaning or word order might prompt the correct word. • If a re-run does not work, ask the child to work on the word and observe the phonic strategies they use. • Use prompts from the guidance in the back of *Collins Big Cat Phonics Readers*. • Listen to the child read every day individually and track their blending ability. • Use the appropriate Benchmark Assessment to match the stage of the programme and follow 'next steps' support. Work in smaller groups – 2–4 maximum. • Keep up the child's confidence and interest in reading by encouraging re-reading of easy books individually, or with a friend.	• Move through the readers and into the main reading programme, working in small groups of up to six. • Teach the child how to break unknown words into syllables and use phonic knowledge of part of the word to help meaning. • Continue to focus on words which might cause problems because they are outside their experience, especially in non-fiction books.
Recognises fast words at once, saying the whole word.	• Use the appropriate Benchmark Assessment to match the stage of the programme and follow next steps support • Listen to the child read every day and track fast word knowledge.	• Move through the readers and into *Collins Big Cat*, working in small groups of up to six.
Decodes words easily, recognises fast words but comprehension is weak.	• If the child is learning English as an additional language, place a bigger focus on words in text which may be unknown and discuss meaning. • Follow the teacher's notes in reading books and work in smaller groups – 2–4 maximum. • Keep up the child's confidence and interest in reading by encouraging re-reading of easy books in pairs and discussing meaning.	(Does not apply.)

Writing assessment support 1

Pupil name _____ Date _____

Typical development and what it looks like	The different writing stages	Tick the stage(s) they are at and comment on their writing	Next steps
			Model writing by the teacher, talking about what they are doing, should be used at ALL stages.
The child's writing is linear – wavy lines across the page, from left to right.	**Emerging:** The child moves their hand across the page 'as if writing'	☐	• The child shares books, pointing at print. • The child dictates captions for pictures to the teacher who scribes.
The child writes separate symbols and letter shapes over a page.	**Emerging:** The child knows that print is needed and is beginning to experiment with symbols and letters.	☐	• The teacher writes with the child, e.g. a shopping list. • The child shares picture dictionaries. • The child looks at print around the room, on packets, etc. • The child looks at a Big Book with the teacher who points to the words, runs their finger under them and says them aloud. • The child copies their name and begins to spot their name amongst the name cards displayed.
The child writes lots of random letters and symbols in linear form, often from left to right.	**Emerging:** The child is beginning to write random letters and symbols across the page, often repeating letters over and over.	☐	• The child recognises their name and 'signs up' for activities. • Groups make and talk about food packaging, letter names and sounds. • The child looks at a Big Book with the teacher who points to the words, runs their finger under them and says them aloud.

Collins Big Cat Phonics Handbook

© HarperCollins*Publishers* 2006. This page may be photocopied for use in the classroom.

Writing assessment support 2

Pupil name _____ Date _____

Typical development and what it looks like	The different writing stages	Tick the stage(s) they are at and comment on their writing	Next steps *Model writing by the teacher, talking about what they are doing, should be used at ALL stages.*
The child writes consistent random letters in a line, often from left to right; they may use capital letters from their name. M b l A n t o 6	**Emerging**: The child is beginning to consistently write random letters and symbols across the page – these may be from their name.	☐	• The teacher scribes for the child who talks about their writing. • The child looks at a Big Book with the teacher who points to the captions, running their finger under the words and saying them aloud. • During the daily phonics session the child begins to link sound to letter shape. • The child uses play opportunities for writing, e.g. labels. • The child can write their own name, sometimes without copying.
The child starts writing letters to represent the first and sometimes the last sound in words; they show some visual memory of fast words, e.g. *the*. e c to s d m Emma came to stay at my h S house	**Developing**: The child is attempting to segment words and can 'hear' and recall the beginning letter, and sometimes the end letters of words. They show some limited recall of fast words.	☐	• In the daily phonics session, the child is developing knowledge of sound/letter links. • The teacher works with individuals on how to use sounds to write words in a simple sentence. • The child looks at a Big Book with the teacher who points to the captions, running their finger under the words and saying them aloud. • The environment encourages lots of play-writing and 'taking risks' with spelling. • Letter charts and words are readily available for children.

Collins Big Cat Phonics Handbook

© HarperCollins*Publishers* 2006. This page may be photocopied for use in the classroom.

Writing assessment support 3

Pupil name _____ Date _____

Typical development and what it looks like	The different writing stages	Tick the stage(s) they are at and comment on their writing	Next steps
			Model writing by the teacher, talking about what they are doing, should be used at ALL stages.
CVC words start to appear in the child's writing; they attempt to write longer words. *Thk you fr The bird tybl*	**Developing:** The child can usually hear sounds along the whole word, in the correct order, and can write each sound. They will also try out longer words, with more than one syllable. They know more fast words and spell them correctly.	☐	• The child has a daily phonics session including a daily writing demonstration. • They read back their own writing to an adult. • The teacher encourages them to 'have a go' and take risks' with spelling. • They confidently 'have a go' and write their own books to read. • Letter charts and words are readily available for them.
The child shows good phonetic spelling and improved recall of fast words. *When I grow up I whant to be a farmer and get a quad and hw a caf and straw*	**Taking off:** The child writes any word that comes into their head confidently, drawing upon the full collection of phonemes. They are willing to experiment with any phoneme that sounds right. They have good fast word knowledge.	☐	• The child has a daily phonics session including a daily writing demonstration with dictation twice a week. • They are encouraged to experiment with different types of writing. • Letter charts and words are readily available for them. • The child will now benefit from some other spelling strategies, e.g. breaking words up into syllables or finding letter patterns in pairs of words.

Ultimate goal: good spelling and very good attitudes to writing. Child takes risks and writes any word that comes into their head with excellent phonic knowledge to back them up.

Observation A

Go to www.collinsbigcat.com to download free phoneme and word lists to use.

Use this to assess one child during a whole class session.

Pupil name _____ Date _____

Phonemes	Blending	Segmenting	Fast words
Circle the correct response.	Tick the box.	Tick the box.	Circle the words they CAN'T read.

Phonemes	Blending	Segmenting	Fast words
s a t i p	**Not at all**	**Not at all**	I
n c k ck e	☐ cvc	☐ cvc	
o r m d g	☐ ccvc	☐ ccvc	the
u l h f b	☐ cvcc	☐ cvcc	
ai j	**Sometimes**	**Sometimes**	to
	☐ cvc	☐ cvc	
	☐ ccvc	☐ ccvc	was
	☐ cvcc	☐ cvcc	
	Consistently	**Consistently**	
	☐ cvc	☐ cvc	
	☐ ccvc	☐ ccvc	
	☐ cvcc	☐ cvcc	

Observation B

Go to www.collinsbigcat.com to download free phoneme and word lists to use.

Use this to assess one child during a whole class session.

Pupil name _____ Date _____

Phonemes	Blending	Segmenting	Fast words
Circle the correct response.	Tick the box.	Tick the box.	Circle the words they CAN'T read.

Phonemes:

s	a	t	i	p
n	c	k	ck	e
o	r	m	d	g
u	l	h	f	b
ai	j	oa	ee	z
w	oo (wood)	oo (cool)	ie	v
y (yak)	ch	sh	th (that)	th (thank)
ng	x	qu	ar	er
ou	oi	ue	or	

Blending:

Not at all
- [ ] cvc   [ ] cvcv
- [ ] ccvc [ ] cvccc
- [ ] cvcc [ ] cccvcc

Sometimes
- [ ] cvc   [ ] cvcv
- [ ] ccvc [ ] cvccc
- [ ] cvcc [ ] cccvcc

Consistently
- [ ] cvc   [ ] cvcv
- [ ] ccvc [ ] cvccc
- [ ] cvcc [ ] cccvcc

Segmenting:

Not at all
- [ ] cvc   [ ] cvcv
- [ ] ccvc [ ] cvccc
- [ ] cvcc [ ] cccvcc

Sometimes
- [ ] cvc   [ ] cvcv
- [ ] ccvc [ ] cvccc
- [ ] cvcc [ ] cccvcc

Consistently
- [ ] cvc   [ ] cvcv
- [ ] ccvc [ ] cvccc
- [ ] cvcc [ ] cccvcc

Fast words:

I	you	like
the	are	no
to	all	have
was	they	be
he	my	by
she	come	one
we	me	so
said	go	some

Collins *Big Cat Phonics Handbook*

Observation C

Go to www.collinsbigcat.com to download free phoneme and word lists to use.

Pupil name _____ Date _____

Use this to assess one child during a whole class session.

Phonemes

Circle the correct response.

s	a	t	i	p	
n	c	k	ck	e	
o	r	m	d	g	
u	l	h	f	b	
ai	j	oa	ee	z	
w	oo (wood)	oo (cool)	ie	v	
y (yak)	ch	sh	th (that)	th (thank)	
ng	x	qu	ar	er	
ou	oi	ue	or	ay	
a-e	ea	y (sunny)	igh	i-e	u-e
y (fly)	ow (snow)	o-e	ew	al	
ir	ur	au	aw	are	
oy	ow (cow)	air			

Blending

Tick the box.

Not at all
- [ ] cvc
- [ ] cvcc
- [ ] ccvc
- [ ] cvcv

Sometimes
- [ ] cvc
- [ ] cvcc
- [ ] ccvc
- [ ] cvcv

Consistently
- [ ] cvc
- [ ] cvcc
- [ ] ccvc
- [ ] cvcv

Segmenting

Tick the box.

Not at all
- [ ] cvc
- [ ] cvcc
- [ ] ccvc
- [ ] cvcv

Sometimes
- [ ] cvc
- [ ] cvcc
- [ ] ccvc
- [ ] cvcv

Consistently
- [ ] cvc
- [ ] cvcc
- [ ] ccvc
- [ ] cvcv

Fast words

Circle the words they CAN'T read.

I	come	her	your
the	me	did	two
to	go	here	very
was	like	there	don't
he	no	saw	people
she	have	when	many
we	be	who	more
said	by	what	could
you	one	where	should
are	so	after	
all	some	because	
they	little	want	
my	do	were	

Collins Big Cat Phonics Handbook

© HarperCollinsPublishers 2006. This page may be photocopied for use in the classroom.

Observation D

Go to www.collinsbigcat.com to download free phoneme and word lists to use.

Use this to assess one child during a whole class session.

Pupil name _____ Date _____

Phonemes

Circle the correct response.

s	a	t	i	p
n	c	k	ck	e
o	r	m	d	g
u	l	h	f	b
ai	j	oa	ee	z
w	oo *(wood)*	oo *(cool)*	ie	v
y *(yak)*	ch	sh	th *(that)*	th *(thank)*
ng	x	qu	ar	er
ou	oi	or	ay	
a-e	ea	y *(sunny)*	igh	i-e
y *(fly)*	ow *(snow)*	o-e	ew	u-e
ir	ur	au	aw	al
oy	ow *(cow)*	air	are	

Blending

Tick the box.

Not at all
- ☐ cvc ☐ cvcv
- ☐ ccvc ☐ cvccc
- ☐ cvcc ☐ cccvcc

Sometimes
- ☐ cvc ☐ cvcv
- ☐ ccvc ☐ cvccc
- ☐ cvcc ☐ cccvcc

Consistently
- ☐ cvc ☐ cvcv
- ☐ ccvc ☐ cvccc
- ☐ cvcc ☐ cccvcc

Segmenting

Tick the box.

Not at all
- ☐ cvc ☐ cvcv
- ☐ ccvc ☐ cvccc
- ☐ cvcc ☐ cccvcc

Sometimes
- ☐ cvc ☐ cvcv
- ☐ ccvc ☐ cvccc
- ☐ cvcc ☐ cccvcc

Consistently
- ☐ cvc ☐ cvcv
- ☐ ccvc ☐ cvccc
- ☐ cvcc ☐ cccvcc

Fast words

Circle the words they CAN'T read.

I	me	here	don't
the	go	there	people
to	like	saw	many
was	no	when	more
he	have	who	could
she	be	what	should
we	by	where	would
said	one	after	put
you	so	because	brother
are	some	want	down
all	little	were	love
they	do	your	their
my	her	two	every
come	did	very	likes

Observation E

Go to www.collinsbigcat.com to download free phoneme and word lists to use.

Use this to assess one child during a whole class session.

Pupil name _____   Date _____

Phonemes
Circle the correct response.

s	a	t	i	p	
n	c	k	ck	e	
o	r	m	d	g	
u	l	h	f	b	
ai	j	oa	ee	z	
w	oo (wood)	oo (cool)			
y (yak)	ch	sh	th (that)	ie	v
ng	x	qu	ar	er	th (thank)
ou	oi	ue	or	ay	
a-e	ea	y (sunny)	igh	i-e	
y (fly)	ow (snow)	o-e	ew	u-e	
ir	ur	au	aw	al	
oy	ow (cow)	air	are		

Blending
Tick the box.

Not at all
- [ ] cvc [ ] cvcv
- [ ] ccvc [ ] cvccc
- [ ] cvcc [ ] cccvcc

Sometimes
- [ ] cvc [ ] cvcv
- [ ] ccvc [ ] cvccc
- [ ] cvcc [ ] cccvcc

Consistently
- [ ] cvc [ ] cvcv
- [ ] ccvc [ ] cvccc
- [ ] cvcc [ ] cccvcc

Segmenting
Tick the box.

Not at all
- [ ] cvc [ ] cvcv
- [ ] ccvc [ ] cvccc
- [ ] cvcc [ ] cccvcc

Sometimes
- [ ] cvc [ ] cvcv
- [ ] ccvc [ ] cvccc
- [ ] cvcc [ ] cccvcc

Consistently
- [ ] cvc [ ] cvcv
- [ ] ccvc [ ] cvccc
- [ ] cvcc [ ] cccvcc

Fast words
Circle the words they CAN'T read.

I	me	here	don't
the	go	there	people
to	like	saw	many
was	no	when	more
he	have	who	could
she	be	what	should
we	by	where	would
said	one	after	put
you	so	because	brother
are	some	want	down
all	little	were	love
they	do	your	their
my	her	two	every
come	did	very	likes

Collins Big Cat Phonics Handbook

© HarperCollinsPublishers 2006. This page may be photocopied for use in the classroom.

Activities

Collins Big Cat Phonics provides seven activities that consolidate the children's new phonic knowledge. When you access the activities from a session, the content will automatically match the level the children have reached in the programme.

The activities can be played by children individually or by one or two teams with an adult as scorer.

The objectives for the activities are taken from the Foundation Stage Early Learning Goals and the Primary National Strategy. On page 31 you can find references to the relevant objectives for each of the activities.

Collins Big Cat Phonics has also been developed to take into account the Primary National Strategy Revised Framework. Visit www.collinsbigcat.com for information on how the programme meets the learning objectives in the new Framework.

Alphabet letter activities

Alphabet Song

Children can sing along with the simple, catchy Alphabet Song (with words by children's poet John Foster) and learn the letters of the alphabet at the same time. As the children sing the song, the letters of the alphabet light up. This activity can be found in the *Alphabet section*.

Letter Shapes

The *Letter Shapes* activity gives children the chance to see the letters of the alphabet drawn in front of them. Simply click on a letter of the alphabet at the bottom of the screen to hear it spoken and see the letter drawn on the screen. Children can join in the demonstration by 'sky-writing' the letters as they appear on the screen. This activity can be found in the *Alphabet section*.

Blending activities for reading

Hide and Seek

The aim of this activity is to read a word to find a hidden Martian. This activity can be completed by children independently. Children listen to a word and click on one of three words on screen to find the Martian. Feedback is given automatically and when children fail to spot the correct word, it is blended for them.

Jack and the Beanstalk

You can play *Jack and the Beanstalk* with the whole class at the whiteboard. Divide the class into two teams and ask them to read the words that appear on the whiteboard. If the team reads the word correctly, click **Jump (✓)**; if they get it wrong click **Stay (✗)**. The team that reaches the bottom of the beanstalk first escapes the giant and wins. When you click **Stay (✗)** the word is blended on screen, demonstrating the correct answer.

Segmenting activities for spelling

Bubbles

Children can do this activity independently to test their segmenting skills. The aim of the activity is to spot the missing phoneme and burst the bubble. Children listen to a word and then see it on screen with one of its phonemes missing. They have to choose between three phonemes to complete the word and burst the bubble. Feedback is given automatically and if children fail to spot the missing phoneme, the word is segmented for them.

Rainbow Letters

In this activity children can build words and sentences by dragging brightly-coloured letters and punctuation marks around the screen. Children can use *Rainbow Letters* to practise forming words and sentences using their phonic knowledge. This activity can be found in the *Alphabet section*.

Reading activities

Treasure Island

Treasure Island tests children's ability to read irregular fast words and regular words by sight. *Treasure Island* can be played at the whiteboard with a group or the whole class. Pick two teams and ask each team to read the word that appears on screen. If the team reads the word correctly, click **Sail (✓)**; if they get it wrong click **Stay (✗)**. The team that reaches the Treasure Island first gets the treasure and wins. When you click **Stay (✗)** the word is read aloud, demonstrating the correct answer.